W9-BFQ-802

MARK

by
J. Vernon McGee

THRU THE BIBLE BOOKS
Box 7100
Pasadena, California 91109

First Printing
1975

Reprints
1980, 1983, 1985

CONTENTS

INTRODUCTION

TIME:

The Gospel of Mark is chronologically the first Gospel that was written. It was actually one of the first books written in the New Testament — not the first, but one of the first. It was probably written from Rome prior to 63 A.D.

THE WRITER

This man Mark was one of the writers of the New Testament who was not actually an apostle. Matthew was an apostle, of course, and so was John. Luke was a very close friend and an intimate of Paul the apostle.

John Mark — *John* was his Jewish name, while *Mark* was his Latin surname (Acts 12:12): "And when he had considered the thing, he came to the house of Mary the mother of John, whose surname was Mark; where many were gathered together praying." (This is referring to the time when Simon Peter was released from prison.) Actually, this is the first historical reference to him that we have in Scripture. Obviously, his mother was a wealthy and prominent Christian in the Jerusalem church and evidently the church there met in her home.

Mark was one who went with Paul on the first missionary journey. He was a nephew of Barnabas. Paul tells us that in Col. 4:10. He evidently was the spiritual son of Simon Peter, because Peter, writing in I Peter 5:13 says, "The church that is at Babylon, elected together with you, saluteth you; and so doth Marcus my son." The Gospel of Mark has long been considered Simon Peter's Gospel. I think there is evidence for that; we'll look at that a little more closely in a moment.

John Mark joined Paul and Barnabas before the first missionary journey. We're told in Acts 13:5: "And when they were at Salamis, they preached the Word of God in the synagogues of the Jews: and they had also John to their minister." But this man turned back at Perga in Pamphylia and apparently it was a fact that he was maybe a little "yellow" or "chicken," as we would say today. I don't think we need to defend John Mark for turning back. He may have had an excuse, but Paul didn't want to take him on the second missionary journey, although Uncle Barnabas did. Barnabas was a great fellow and was ready to forgive; but not Paul. In Acts 15:37,38 I read, "And Barnabas determined to take with them John, whose surname was Mark. But Paul thought not good to take him with them, who departed from them from Pamphylia and went not with them to the work." Now, that looks to me like Paul thought he had failed. We're told in verse 39 of that chapter, "And the contention was so sharp between them, that they departed asunder one from the other: and so Barnabas took Mark, and sailed unto Cyprus." As far as we are concerned, he sails right off the pages of Scripture. We know very little about the ministry of John Mark.

We do know that John Mark made good. When Paul wrote his swan song in II Tim. 4:11 he says, "Only Luke is with me. Take Mark, and bring him with thee: for he is profitable for me for the ministry."

There has always been a question of whether he is mentioned somewhere in the Gospel record. While I call attention to it, I personally do not think that there is any basis to that supposition at all.

We are told that this man, Mark, got his *facts* of the Gospel from Peter. Others say that he got the *explanation* of the Gospel from Paul. I'm willing to accept that.

TO WHOM WRITTEN

Why are there four Gospels? One reason is that they were written to different people. Matthew was written for the nation Israel; it was written for the religious man. Mark was written specifically for the Roman, and it was suited for the Roman times. It was written for the strong man. The Romans ruled the world for a millennium. The Gospel of Mark was written for such people. The Romans actually had subjugated the world; they had brought peace and justice, good roads, law and order, protection; but it was a forced peace. The iron heel of Rome was on mankind and it had to pay a price. Rome was a strong dictatorship. Dr. D. S. Gregory has expressed it like this: "[The

Roman] was to try whether human power, taking the form of law, regulated by political principles of which a regard for law and justice was most conspicuous, could perfect humanity by subordinating the individual to the state and making the state universal." Dr. Robert Culver, in his book on Daniel, says that the Roman gave to the world the kind of peace that the League of Nations and now the United Nations tries to give to the world. This kind of peace has already been tried by the Romans and it must be a peace that is pushed down on the world, forced on the world, and held in the hands of a very strong man. The world today, of course, is looking again for that strong man to come along.

Rome represented active, human power in the ancient world, and it led to dictatorship. The power was actually vested in one man, which, of course, was the thing that was dangerous. Again that is the danger today, as we are moving in that direction. I'd like to quote Dr. D. S. Gregory again in this connection. "The grandest Roman, the ideal man of the race, was therefore the mightiest worker, conqueror, organizer, and ruler, — the man who as *Caesar* could sway the sceptre of the universal empire. Caesar and Caesarism were the inevitable result of Roman development . . . . When [the Roman] had been made to feel most deeply that natural justice in the hands of a human despot is a dreadful thing for sinful man, — the Holy Ghost proposes to commend to his acceptance Jesus of Nazareth as his Sovereign and Saviour, the expected deliverer of the world." We're moving into a position today where there will come a police state, ruled by one man. He'll be satanic, ruling over sinful men so that they will cry out for deliverance. The only One who will be able to deliver will be the Lord Jesus Christ when He comes!

Paul wrote to the Romans, "I am not ashamed of the gospel of Christ: for it is the power of God unto salvation to every one that believeth" (Romans 1:16). That power is the power that can extend mercy. In the days when the Caesars ruled, the world longed for mercy and all they got was power. It was a day in which no man dared to resist that power because to resist it was fatal. To flee from it was impossible — one could never get beyond it. It was in that day that God sent a message to that segment of the population, and John Mark is the writer.

John Mark is giving Simon Peter's account of the Gospel. The early church felt that this was true and took that position. For example, Papias, one of the early church fathers, recorded that John Mark got his Gospel from Simon Peter: "Mark, the interpreter of Peter, wrote carefully down all that he recollected, but not according to the order of Christ's speaking or working." Eusebius says that "such a light of piety shone into the minds of those who heard Peter that they were not satisfied with once hearing, nor with the unwritten doctrine that was delivered, but earnestly besought Mark (whose Gospel is now spread abroad) that he would leave in writing for them the doctrine which they had received by preaching." So it was, therefore, that we got Simon Peter's Gospel through John Mark.

CHARACTERISTICS OF MARK'S GOSPEL

It is a Gospel of action because Simon Peter was that kind of man. It is a Gospel of action, written to the Roman who was also a man of action.

In Mark's Gospel, Jesus lays aside the regal robes of kingship and girds Himself with the towel of service. He is King in Matthew's Gospel; He is the Servant in the Gospel of Mark. But He is not man's servant; He is God's Servant. Mark expresses it by stating the words of our Lord, "For even the Son of man came not to be ministered unto, but to minister, and to give his life a ransom for many" (Mark 10:45).

In Mark's Gospel Jesus is presented as the Servant of Jehovah. This fulfills Isaiah 42:1,2: "Behold my servant, whom I uphold: mine elect, in whom my soul delighteth; I have put my spirit upon him: he shall bring forth judgment to the Gentiles. He shall not cry, nor lift up, nor cause his voice to be heard in the street."

Bernard, way back in 1864, said of the Gospel of Mark: "St. Peter's saying to Cornelius has been well noticed as a fit motto for this Gospel: 'God anointed Jesus of Nazareth with the Holy Ghost and with power; who went about doing good and healing all those who were oppressed of the devil.' "

Someone has put it like this:

> I read
> In a book
> Where a man called
> Christ
> Went about doing good.
> It is very disconcerting
> To me
> That I am so easily
> Satisfied
> With just
> Going about.

We read a great deal today about protesting and marches, and we hear about do-gooders, both the politicians and the preachers. They all *talk* about doing good, but they are just going about. The Lord Jesus came in the winsomeness of His humanity and the fulness of His deity doing good. This was only the beginning of the Gospel. He died and rose again. Then He said to His own, "Go." The Gospel was then completed. This is the Gospel today.

The style of Mark is brief and blunt, pertinent and pithy, short and sweet. Mark is stripped of excess verbiage and goes right to the point. This is the Gospel of action and accomplishment. Here Jesus is not adorned with words and narrative but He is stripped and girded for action.

Mark is written in a simple style. It is designed for the masses of the street. It is interesting to note that the connective *and* occurs more than any other word in the Gospel. It is said to occur 1,331 times. I didn't count that, friends, but if you doubt that statement, you count them. Very frankly, if I had turned in a college English paper with that many *and's* in it, I would have been flunked. Yet it is a potent word when it is used correctly. It is a word of action and it means something must follow. I've heard a lot of speakers, especially young preachers, and when they are reaching for something to say they will use the word *and*. The minute they say that, my friends, they've got to say something else. No sentence can end with *and*. *And* always leads to further action.

Mark wrote this Gospel, I believe, in Rome, evidently for Romans, because they were a busy people and believed in power and action. They wanted the answer to this question: *Is Jesus able to do the job?* This Gospel is brief enough for a busy man to read. Few Old Testament Scriptures are quoted and Jewish customs are explained which give additional proof that it was written for foreigners.

Matthew gives to us a genealogy because a king must have a genealogy. Mark does not give one because a servant doesn't need a genealogy, he needs references. A servant needs to do the job. We're going to see that in this Gospel because that is the way Jesus is presented.

OUTLINE

The Credentials of Christ

I. John INTRODUCES the Servant, 1:1-8
   (Death of John, 6:14-29)

II. God the Father IDENTIFIES the Servant, 1:9-11
   (9:1-8, Transfiguration)

III. The Temptation INITIATES the Servant, 1:12, 13

IV. Works and Words ILLUSTRATE (Illumine)
   the Servant, 1:14-13:37

   1. Miracles

   (1) *Healing (Physical)*
      (i) Peter's Wife's Mother (fever), and Others, 1:29-34
      (ii) Leper, 1:40-45
      (iii) Palsied Man Let Down Through Roof, 2:1-12
      (iv) Man with Withered Hand, 3:1-5
      (v) Many Healed by Sea of Galilee, 3:6-10
      (vi) Woman with Issue of Blood, 5:21-34
      (vii) Sick at Nazareth, 6:5
      (viii) Disciples Heal, 6:13
      (ix) Sick in Land of Gennesaret, 6:53-56
      (x) Deaf and Dumb of Decapolis, 7:31-37
      (xi) Blind Man of Bethsaida, 8:22-26
      (xii) Blind Bartimaeus, 10:46-52

   (2) *Nature (Natural)*
      (i) Stills the Storm, 4:35-41
      (ii) Five Thousand Fed, 6:32-44
      (iii) Walks on Sea, 6:45-52
      (iv) Four Thousand Fed, 8:1-9
      (v) Fig Tree Cursed, 11:12-14

   (3) *Demons (Spiritual)*
      (i) Man in Synagogue, 1:21-27
      (ii) Many Demons in Capernaum, 1:32-34
      (iii) Demons in Galilee, 1:39
      (iv) Unclean Spirits by Sea of Galilee, 3:11, 12

CHAPTER 1

There probably is more content in this first chapter of Mark than any other chapter in the Bible (compare with Genesis 1). It covers the ministry of John the Baptist, after going back to the prophecies of Isaiah and Malachi. It takes in the first year's ministry of Jesus, and follows Him through a busy Sabbath day. It concludes with the mighty work of cleansing the leper. In spite of the pressure of a busy life, Jesus took time to pray.

This chapter of crowded content is made striking by the absence of genealogy which is so prominent in Matthew. We have already stated why. A king must have a genealogy. A servant needs references, not a "birth certificate." It is not a question as to His ancestors, rather as to His actions — can He do the job? Jehovah's Servant is marked out here by His accomplishments. Besides this, the Romans or other outsiders would not be concerned with the genealogy of Jesus, which is traced back to Abraham.

As we begin the text of this Gospel, let us ask God to bring us into vital relationship with Jesus. We are going to behold the Lord Jesus Christ. Dr. A. J. Gordon wrote: "The look saves but the gaze sanctifies."

The beginning of the gospel of Jesus Christ, the Son of God:

As it is written in the prophets, Behold, I send my messenger before thy face, which shall prepare thy way before thee.

The voice of one crying in the wilderness, Prepare ye the way of the Lord, make his paths straight [Mark 1:1-3].

This is not the beginning of either John or Jesus. It is the beginning of the Gospel when the Lord Jesus came to this earth and died upon a cross and rose again. That, my friend, is the Gospel.

There are three beginnings recorded in Scripture. Let us put them down in chronological order:

1. "In the beginning was the Word . . ." (John 1:1). This goes back to a dateless beginning, a beginning before all time. Here the human mind can only grope. It is logical rather than chronological because in my thinking, I must put my peg somewhere in the past in order to take off. If I see an airplane in the air, I assume there is an airport somewhere. I may not know where it is but I know the plane took off from some place. So when I look around at the universe, I know that it took off from somewhere and that somewhere there is a God. But I don't know anything about that beginning. God comes out of eternity to meet us. I just have to put down the pegs at the point where He does meet us, back as far as I can think, and realize He was there before that.

2. "In the beginning God created the heaven and the earth" (Gen. 1:1). This is where we move out of eternity into time. However, although many people have been attempting to date this universe, no man so far knows. Man's guesses have ranged from six thousand to three billions of years. We know so little but when we come into His presence and begin to know even as we are known, then we will realize how we saw through a glass darkly. I'm sure we will marvel at our stupidity and our ignorance. Our God is a great God. He has plenty of time.

3. "The beginning of the gospel" (Mark 1:1) is the same as "That which was from the beginning . . ." (I John 1:1). This is dated. It goes back to Jesus Christ at the precise moment He took upon Himself human flesh. Jesus Christ is the Gospel!

Then Mark, who has very few quotations from the Old Testament, quotes two prophecies. The Romans knew very little about prophecy but he does this to show them that this One whom he is talking about doesn't need a genealogy but he does need references. So Mark shows that His references go back to Isaiah and to Malachi. Both John and Mark declare that the coming of John the Baptist fulfilled the prophecies of the one who would be the forerunner of Christ.

John did baptize in the wilderness, and preach the baptism of repentance for the remission of sins [Mark 1:4].

I want to change the wording so that we can get the meaning of this verse. John preached repentance and baptized *unto* remission for sins, not *for* remission of sins. The Greek preposition *eis* is used with *remission*, and is translated "unto" or "into." His ministry was preparatory. It was preparing them for the coming of the Lord Jesus Christ into the world. Jesus Christ is the One who remits sins.

> **And there went out unto him all the land of Judaea, and they of Jerusalem, and were all baptized of him in the river of Jordan, confessing their sins.**

> **And John was clothed with camel's hair, and with a girdle of a skin about his loins; and he did eat locusts and wild honey [Mark 1:5, 6]**

John the Baptist was remarkable, not only in his message, but remarkable in his dress and in his diet. This man was one who had been set aside for this ministry. He was of the order of the priests, a Levite, and was expected to minister in the temple in Jerusalem. But God had called him as a prophet, and he is out in the wilderness preaching. And the people come out to hear him!

Today, we like to put a church in a location where people live or where they can congregate and come together. We feel that the church should be accessible. John didn't work on that theory at all. He was way out yonder in the wilderness and the multitudes went out to him.

> **And preached, saying, There cometh one mightier than I after me, the latchet of whose shoes I am not worthy to stoop down and unloose [Mark 1:7].**

This reveals something of how remarkable this man really was. He stirred the multitudes. He was a strange and a strong man, but his was a solo voice. Notice his humility. John the Baptist was an humble man.

> **I indeed have baptized you with water: but he shall baptize you with the Holy Ghost [Mark 1:8].**

This is the great distinction between John and Jesus. The *real* baptism is the baptism with the Holy Spirit. *Ritual* baptism is by water. Water baptism is very important today because it is a testimony. In the Gospel of Matthew we learned that the reason the Lord Jesus was baptized was actually to identify Himself with mankind.

> **And it came to pass in those days, that Jesus came from Nazareth of Galilee, and was baptized of John in Jordan [Mark 1:9].**

Notice Mark's headline — "JESUS CAME." What a thrill! Jesus is coming again someday. That's another wonderful headline. But here, the Lord Jesus came from the obscurity of thirty years of quiet training in little Nazareth. He comes now and identifies Himself with the human family in His baptism. You remember that Jesus had said to John, "Suffer it to be so now" (Matthew 3:15), because John didn't think he should baptize Jesus.

Notice also that His name "Jesus" is used here. Jesus came. We will find that it is His common name that is used in this Gospel. The name *Jesus* is used more frequently in Mark than any other name.

> **And straightway coming up out of the water, he saw the heavens opened, and the Spirit like a dove descending upon him:**

> **And there came a voice from heaven, saying, Thou art my beloved Son, in whom I am well pleased [Mark 1:10, 11].**

Here we see the Trinity brought together in a very definite way. We see the Lord Jesus, the second Person of the Godhead; the Spirit of God who descends like a dove upon Him — the Spirit is the third Person of the Godhead; and the voice from heaven saying, "Thou art my beloved Son" is that of the Father, the first Person of the Godhead. So the Trinity is brought to our attention. And this, by the way, is heaven's seal upon the Person and dedication of Jesus.

You will notice that things are happening very fast here. He is the Servant. John the Baptist is the one who introduces Him and then God the Father identifies Him and puts His seal upon Him. Next the temptation will initiate Him.

And immediately the spirit driveth him into the wilderness [Mark 1:12].

Driveth is a word of fierceness and seriousness. The Spirit of God moved Him right out into the wilderness that He might be tempted. This is something that is very important for us to see. We come again to that question: Can He do the job? Other men had failed; they couldn't stand up under temptation. Adam failed. Noah got through the Flood and then he miserably fell on his face. We saw that Abraham failed. Moses failed — he led the children of Israel out of Egypt but he wasn't permitted to enter the Promised Land. And poor David failed. So we see that the temptation initiates Him into His work.

And he was there in the wilderness forty days, tempted of Satan; and was with the wild beasts; and the angels ministered unto him [Mark 1:13].

We do not have the detail given here that we find in Matthew and in Luke. He was in the wilderness forty days, tempted of Satan. He was tempted during the whole forty days. Some people seem to have the impression that he fasted forty days and then Satan tempted Him. My friend, He was being tempted all the time.

Some people have the idea that He was there tempted of Satan and that the wild beasts more or less contributed to the temptation. Mark is saying here that He was with the wild beasts and the angels and they both ministered to Him. The beasts are a part of creation put under the dominion of man. That's the reason God created these creatures. Remember in Genesis we learned that everything was a preparation to make a home for man. As far as we know, this earth is the only place in which there is mankind and which is habitable for man. Here, the beasts which were below the Man Christ Jesus ministered to Him, and the angels above Him ministered to Him. That is what Mark is saying here.

Now after that John was put in prison, Jesus came into Galilee, preaching the gospel of the kingdom of God,

And saying, The time is fulfilled, and the kingdom of

God is at hand: repent ye, and believe the gospel [Mark 1:14, 15].

After the temptation, we find Jesus beginning His ministry. Notice again Mark's flaming headline: JESUS CAME. After John the Baptist was imprisoned, Jesus came into Galilee. He begins His ministry now, preaching the Gospel of God, saying, The time is fulfilled and the Kingdom of God is at hand.

"Of the kingdom" is not in the better manuscripts and I, personally, think it should be "preaching the *gospel of God* and saying, The time is fulfilled . . ." The Gospel of God is that the Kingdom of God is at hand. In Matthew it was the "Kingdom of Heaven." Is there a distinction between the two? Yes, there is, and there is also an overlapping. The Kingdom of Heaven is God's rule over the earth; the Kingdom of God includes His entire universe, even beyond the bounds of this earth. So the Kingdom of Heaven is *in* the Kingdom of God. Matthew is applying God's rule specifically to this earth. Mark is reaching out and including a wider area because the Kingdom of God includes the entire universe with all of His creatures. As far as the earth is concerned, to say "the kingdom of heaven is at hand" or "the kingdom of God is at hand" would be synonymous. But the Kingdom of God would include regions beyond the earth while the Kingdom of Heaven means the reign of the heavens over the earth.

The message of Jesus is the same as the message of John the Baptist in Matthew's Gospel. "Repent ye and believe the gospel." I believe that in our day, the message is really turned around — that is, we put faith before repentance. When you turn to Jesus Christ in faith, you are actually turning *to* Him *from* something else, and that turning *from* something is repentance. If there was not that turning *from* something, then apparently there was not a real turning *to* Christ. It is true that if there is a real turning to Christ, there will be a manifestation of a change in the life showing that the believer is turning from something. So there is no contradiction at all. The important thing is for the people to believe in the Gospel.

We are seeing fast action here, but remember, this Gospel is written for the Romans who were men of action. They were men of power who ruled the world. Matthew is directed to the religious man. Mark was written to the strong man. Luke is addressed to the thinking man. The Gospel of John is directed to the wretched man, the man who needs salvation.

> Now as he walked by the sea of Galilee, he saw Simon and Andrew his brother casting a net into the sea; for they were fishers.
>
> And Jesus said unto them, Come ye after me, and I will make you to become fishers of men.
>
> And straightway they forsook their nets, and followed him.
>
> And when he had gone a little farther thence, he saw James the son of Zebedee, and John his brother, who also were in the ship mending their nets.
>
> And straightway he called them: and they left their father Zebedee in the ship with the hired servants, and went after him [Mark 1:16-20].

There were three separate and distinct calls made to the Apostles:

1. In John 1:35-51 we are told that when He went up to Jerusalem He met these men and gave them a general call, informal and casual. They wanted to know where He lived because John the Baptist had marked Him out, and some of John's disciples followed Him. But they didn't stay with Him — He didn't ask them to at this time. They went back to their fishing in Galilee.

2. Now, we find here in Mark that at the beginning of His ministry, He walks along the sea and finds the disciples fishing, and He calls them to discipleship. They are to be "fishers of men." However, we find in Luke 5:1-11 that again they went back to their fishing.

3. The final call was a call to apostleship. It is recorded in Mark 3 and in Matthew 10 and Luke 6. They had gone back to fishing, and Simon Peter said to Him, "Depart from me, Lord, for I am a sinful man." What he is really saying is, "Why don't you go and get somebody else. Let me alone because I have failed

you so — I'm a sinful man." But the Lord didn't give him up;
thank God for that. So the Lord came to them the third time and
appointed them to apostleship.

**And they went into Capernaum; and straightway on the
sabbath day he entered into the synagogue, and taught
[Mark 1:21].**

You will remember that when the religious leaders would question Him about what He did on the Sabbath day, He would
make it very clear, "My Father worketh hitherto, and I work"
(John 5:17). We are going to see that He didn't work an eight-
hour day — "He that keepeth Israel shall neither slumber nor
sleep" (Psalm 121:4). This Sabbath day starts out early in the
morning when He entered into the synagogue and taught. This
synagogue in Capernaum was not a center of vital religion in that
day. It seems that He left Nazareth because His own people
would not receive Him and He went down to Capernaum which
He made His headquarters all during His earthly ministry.

**And they were astonished at his doctrine: for he taught
them as one that had authority, and not as the
scribes [Mark 1:22].**

Here we see the effect of the potency of truth and the manner
of this Man. This criticism against the church today and against
the ministry is that we do not speak with authority. The reason
the ministry does not speak with authority is that we have lost
our faith. When I say "we," I do not mean I have lost my faith. I
mean that as a class, the ministry today does not attempt to
preach and to teach the Word of God. There is a departure from
the truth and a tremendous bifurcation between the pulpit and
the Word of God. The synagogue offered nothing vital in that
day, and as a result, when our Lord spoke, they were astonished
at His doctrine.

**And there was in their synagogue a man with an unclean
spirit; and he he cried out,**

**Saying, Let us alone; what have we to do with thee, thou
Jesus of Nazareth? art thou come to destroy us? I know
thee who thou art, the Holy One of God [Mark 1:23, 24].**

This first miracle in the Gospel of Mark is in the spiritual realm. God only is in control in the spiritual realm; He is in control of the demons. There is a great deal of historical evidence that demonism was rampant in the entire Roman Empire. The only way demonism can be met is by the Lord Jesus because He, and He alone, is able to move in this realm. That is the reason Mark gives this as the first miracle. He brings this miracle first because if Jesus has power in this realm, then there are two things that are implied. First, He has power in any realm. Second, only God could do such a thing. This was a part of His credentials, you see. He had authority; He had power. He taught as One who had authority, and now He demonstrates that He has power.

If you are aware of what is taking place in our contemporary culture today, you recognize that Satan worship has become very prominent. There are things happening today in the realm of the occult that can be explained only on the basis that it is satanic and that it is supernatural. You cannot explain reasonably why young people today will leave homes where they are loved, join a vagrant band, and then go out and murder! That seems unbelievable. That's satanic, friends. And we're going to see actual demon possession if this continues.

Christian friend, there is only one way to deal with this, and that is in the name of the Lord Jesus Christ. He alone can control the demons. That is the first miracle that is given to us in Mark.

And Jesus rebuked him, saying, Hold thy peace, and come out of him.

And when the unclean spirit had torn him, and cried with a loud voice, he came out of him.

And they were all amazed, insomuch that they questioned among themselves, saying, What thing is this? what new doctrine is this? for with authority commandeth he even the unclean spirits, and they do obey him [Mark 1:25-27].

Notice, friends, He is demonstrating His power and His authority in His teaching and in His miracles and they cannot understand it. He has authority which they cannot comprehend.

> **And immediately his fame spread abroad throughout all the region round about Galilee [Mark 1:28].**

Mark takes us on to the next incident which evidently took place the same day but sometime in the afternoon.

> **And forthwith, when they were come out of the synagogue, they entered into the house of Simon and Andrew, with James and John.**
>
> **But Simon's wife's mother lay sick of a fever, and anon they tell him of her.**
>
> **And he came and took her by the hand, and lifted her up; and immediately the fever left her, and she ministered unto them [Mark 1:29-31].**

She's not called a mother-in-law, she's called Simon's wife's mother. My own mother-in-law used to call this to my attention. She thought this was a nice way of saying it, and I'm sure it is. So here was another miracle which He performed that same day. Then we follow Him on into the evening.

> **And at even, when the sun did set, they brought unto him all that were diseased, and them that were possessed with demons [Mark 1:32].**

I am sure you recognize that "devils" in the King James Version should be translated *demons*. There is only one devil, who is Satan, but there are many demons, as we shall see.

> **And all the city was gathered together at the door.**
>
> **And he healed many that were sick of divers diseases, and cast out many demons, and suffered not the demons to speak, because they knew him [Mark 1:33, 34].**

Now Mark is doing precisely the same thing that Matthew did. He calls our attention to the fact that he tells us only very few incidents of Jesus' healing. He literally healed hundreds and hundreds of people, but only a few isolated incidents are recorded for us.

It is interesting to note that the demon world recognized Him.

They knew and believed who He was, and yet they are not saved, of course.

We've gone through a busy day with Him, and you would think that after such an exhausting Sabbath day, He would sleep late the next morning. But we read:

> **And in the morning, rising up a great while before day, he went out, and departed into a solitary place, and there prayed [Mark 1:35].**

You would think that after that busy Sabbath day, He would relax the next day. I know a lot of preachers take Monday off after a busy Sunday. I don't blame them for that. I formerly did it myself, but I haven't done it for quite a few years now. No, we see Jesus rising up early to go to a solitary place to pray. What a lesson this is for us.

> **And Simon and they that were with him followed after him. And when they had found him, they said unto him, All men seek for thee.**
>
> **And he said unto them, Let us go into the next towns, that I may preach there also: for therefore came I forth.**
>
> **And he preached in their synagogues throughout all Galilee, and cast out devils [Mark 1:36-39].**

This is the beginning of the gospel, you see, for by His teaching He is preparing them for that which is salvation; that is, His death and His resurrection. His teaching will not save you, friends, but rather it is His work on the cross that saves us.

Notice that He preached in their synagogues and cast out demons throughout all Galilee. He covers that entire territory in His three years of ministry.

Again we note that there was a great manifestation of demon power at this time. There are three such periods: one was during the time of Moses, one was during the time of Elijah, and one was during the time of our Lord here on earth.

We come, now, to the last miracle of the chapter. All of these have been hard cases and they all have been different. This one is a leper. Leprosy was not incurable, as we shall see in Leviticus, but it was a disease that could be fatal. It was certainly a tragic disease as it deformed and mutilated the victim and barred him from society.

> And there came a leper to him, beseeching him, and kneeling down to him, and saying unto him, If thou wilt, thou canst make me clean.

> And Jesus, moved with compassion, put forth his hand, and touched him, and saith unto him, I will; be thou clean [Mark 1:40, 41].

There is a tremendous psychological side to this miracle. One doesn't touch a leper. This man hadn't been touched in many years. Nor had he been able to touch anyone. I imagine his family brought out the food and drink for him, left it, and after they had retired he would come up and get it. He probably could wave to them, but he could never come to them again, never hold them in his arms, never touch them. But now the Lord *touches* this man, and He cleanses him!

> And as soon as he had spoken, immediately the leprosy departed from him, and he was cleansed.

> And he straitly charged him, and forthwith sent him away;

> And saith unto him, See thou say nothing to any man: but go thy way, shew thyself to the priest, and offer for thy cleansing those things which Moses commanded, for a testimony unto them [Mark 1:42-44].

The cleansing of a leper was to follow a Mosaic ritual. Our Lord did not break the Mosaic Law.

> But he went out, and began to publish it much, and to blaze abroad the matter, insomuch that Jesus could no more openly enter into the city, but was without in desert places: and they came to him from every quarter [Mark 1:45].

This man, instead of keeping quiet about it, went out and published it. If you want to get a thing out, publish it, put it in the paper or on the radio. That's what this man did. To "blaze" abroad means to set something on fire like a forest fire. Friends, if you are having trouble getting your neighbors to listen to you, just set your place on fire! I can assure you that the whole neighborhood will come around you.

Some years ago I was holding meetings in a church in Prescott, Arizona, and I casually remarked to the preacher, "If you want to get a crowd here this week, set the place on fire." Do you know that when I was preaching on Sunday night he got up, walked out in the Sunday School department, came back in, pushed me aside, and said, "Friends, the church is on fire." He asked them to file out in an orderly way, and by then we could hear the sirens and the fire engines coming. Now I tell you, we had a good crowd all week. The announcement of the meeting had been on the back pages of the newspaper, but on Monday, it was on the front page with the account of the fire at the church and the assurance that the meetings would go on. So the crowds came all week. After that I recommended to every preacher who was going to hold meetings that he set the place on fire. That's one way to get a crowd.

So this healed man blazed abroad the news. He disobeyed our Lord, however. I used to go over after I had finished preaching, to help preach for a black man, a very wonderful preacher in Texas. I got over there one evening before he had finished preaching, and I want to tell you, he said one of the wisest things I've heard about this. Preaching on this section of the Gospel of Mark, he said, "The Lord told him not to tell anybody and he told everybody. He tells us to tell everybody and we tell nobody." I thought that was good. I want to say, friends, the disobedience of this cleansed leper is not as bad as our disobedience today. We are to tell everybody and we tell nobody.

However, because he blazed abroad the news, the crowds came, and our Lord had to withdraw from Capernaum for a time.

CHAPTER 2

Chapter 2 is another chapter filled with action. It is really a continuation of chapter 1, beginning with that marvelous connective "and" that Mark uses so often. It's the little word that is the cement that holds this Gospel together. It always joins what has gone before with what is to follow.

And again he entered into Capernaum after some days; and it was noised that he was in the house [Mark 2:1].

We see that He entered into Capernaum after some days. I think we said last time that He had moved His headquarters from His home town of Nazareth down to Capernaum. The best I can tell is that Capernaum remained the headquarters for our Lord's earthly ministry of three years.

We saw last time that He had to withdraw into desert places because the leper whom He had healed didn't obey what Jesus had requested him to do, but had gone out and told everyone. So then the crowds pushed upon Him and our Lord couldn't do His work.

This is one of several reasons why the Lord Jesus did not come as a thaumaturgist, a wonder worker. He didn't want that to be the thing that would characterize Him. He didn't want this man and others to tell about His miracles because He had come for a spiritual ministry. He had come to die upon the cross for the sins of the world. This type of publicity obscures the Gospel.

Very candidly, and I want to be fair and frank, one of the reasons that I object so vociferously today to these people who put the emphasis on healing or tongues or something like that is that, even if these were gifts for this age in which we are living, it is getting the cart before the horse. Someone said to me some time ago, "Well, Dr. McGee, So-and-So preaches the Gospel, just like you do, and he has a healing ministry too." Yes, but is he known for preaching the Gospel? Is that the reason people go to the meetings? Do they go to hear the Gospel to be saved or is the emphasis upon healing or some other emotional experience? I think we need today to whittle this down to a very fine point. Our business is primarily to preach the Gospel. We see here in Mark's Gospel that our Lord was hindered so much because of this sensation over the leper that He left Capernaum for a while (we don't know how long) and then came back again.

When He came back, it says it was noised that He was in the house. The little Greek word *the* is really an adjective in the Greek and it is so declined. It is a modifier to the word *house* and refers to a very definite, particular house. So the question is: Which house is mentioned in the first chapter of this Gospel? In the first chapter we are told that after He had been to the synagogue that morning, He entered into the house of Simon and Andrew. This leads us to believe that when these fellows start taking off the roof, they are taking the roof off Simon Peter's house! It's hard to imagine Peter being docile and standing aside to let them do it. Not Simon Peter! I have a notion that he even threatened them with the police. It was his house.

The word got around that our Lord had come back to Capernaum and that He was at Simon Peter's house.

And straightway many were gathered together, insomuch that there was no room to receive them, no, not so much as about the door: and he preached the word unto them [Mark 2:2].

The ministry of our Lord was to preach the Word of God, and that is the emphasis that we feel should be made today. It is the emphasis upon the Word of God, upon the integrity and inerrancy of the Word of God. My prayer for myself in this connection is, "Oh God, give me more confidence in the Word of God." I see what it is doing today in hearts and lives and I know what it has done for me. As a result, I should have even more confidence than I have. I'll be very frank with you; sometimes I wonder whether it is going to have any influence in any heart or life. I must confess that I don't have the faith that I should have. We must remember that this is the Word of God and it will never return unto Him void (Isaiah 55:11). So I rejoice to read here that our Lord preached the Word unto them.

Now our attention is directed to another group. It consists of a little delegation of five. They are coming down the dusty road to Capernaum.

> **And they come unto him, bringing one sick of the palsy, which was borne of four.**

> **And when they could not come nigh unto him for the press, they uncovered the roof where he was: and when they had broken it up, they let down the bed wherein the sick of the palsy lay [Mark 2:3, 4].**

Our attention is directed to this little group of five and this is how they look. One man is sick with the palsy, poor fellow. He couldn't even have made it there because he's in that stretcher. The other four make a kind of quartet, one at each corner of the stretcher. And here they come. They can't get in because of the crowd which actually fills the doors and the windows.

Now, I've found in church work today that the thing that is done more than anything else is to designate committees. The committee is what the pastor of a church often depends on. Church work, today, is done largely by the committees of various organizations. Someone has said that a committee is made up of those who take down minutes and waste hours. Another has said that a committee is made up of a group of people who individually can do nothing, but together they can decide that nothing can be done. And that is generally what they do.

If they did it like we do it, this little group had a committee. They had a door committee who came up and looked around and then went back and said, "You can't get in the door." Then they had the window committee who went up and looked around and came back and said, "You can't get in a window." Fortunately, they had a roof committee, and the roof committee came back and said, "We think we can get him down through the roof." So, maybe, if you have enough committees, there will be one that will function.

Anyway, they decided to let him down through the roof, and so these men tackle the job of taking off the roof. When they get him down into the presence of Christ, I think they are embarrassed because they see they have broken up the meeting. You can imagine what it did for the meeting in progress! We have no notion what the Lord was teaching on this occasion, but it came to a sudden halt. But our Lord must have looked at them and smiled — I'm almost sure that He did.

When Jesus saw their faith, he said unto the sick of the palsy, Son, thy sins be forgiven thee [Mark 2:5].

Whose faith? It was the faith of these men. That disturbed me for quite a few years whenever I looked at this verse. It seemed to me that it was the faith of these men that was responsible for him being saved. "Thy sins be forgiven thee." But as I studied it, I realized that it was not *their* faith that saved him.

It's wonderful to have a godly mother, but you are not going to heaven tied to your mamma's apron strings. It's wonderful to have a godly father, but your godly father won't save you. You will have to exert faith yourself. *You* must be the believing one.

On closer examination we see that it is not the faith of these four men that saved this man. It was the faith of these men that brought him to the place where he could hear the Lord Jesus deal with him individually and personally. "When Jesus saw their faith" means their faith to bring the palsied man to Him. When He saw this, then He dealt personally with the man and said, "Son, thy sins be forgiven thee."

What we need in the church today is stretcher-bearers — men and women with that kind of faith to go out and bring in the unsaved so they can hear the Gospel. There are many people today who are paralyzed with a palsy of sin, a palsy of indifference, or a palsy of prejudice. A great many people are not going to come into church where the Gospel is preached unless you take a corner of the stretcher and bring them in. That's what these men did. They had the faith to bring this poor man to hear the Lord Jesus deal with him personally and say, "Son, thy sins be forgiven thee."

But there were certain of the scribes sitting there, and reasoning in their hearts,

Why doth this man thus speak blasphemies? who can forgive sins but God only? [Mark 2:6,7].

Here's the enemy and they don't speak out but just think their thoughts. In their thinking, they are wrong on the first question, but they are right in the second question. This Man was not speaking blasphemies. But it is true that only God can forgive sin.

No judge has any right to let a criminal off. His business is to enforce the law. God is the moral ruler of this universe and He must defend His own laws. God cannot be lawless. He can't be, because He is righteous. Having made the laws, He obeys those laws and His laws are inexorable. They are not changed at all, and by them you and I are guilty before God. We need forgiveness of our sins and He does forgive. Let us never make the mistake of thinking He forgives because He is big-hearted. He forgives us because Christ paid the penalty for our sins! The Lord Jesus was not speaking blasphemies — He *is* God. And He could forgive sins because He came to this earth to provide a salvation for you and me and for the man with the palsy.

And immediately when Jesus perceived in his spirit that they so reasoned within themselves, he said unto them, Why reason ye these things in your hearts? [Mark 2:8].

These men didn't speak out, you see, but they thought this in their hearts. He tries to draw them out but these men had had a run-in with Him before and they had always come away with a bloody nose. So they decided the best thing to do here was to keep quiet, and they did. So our Lord said to them,

Whether is it easier to say to the sick of the palsy, Thy sins be forgiven thee; or to say, Arise, and take up thy bed, and walk? [Mark 2:9].

By the way, they're not about to answer that one at all. They're quiet and since they are quiet, He is still going to deal with them. He knew what they were thinking. In the Gospel of John 2:25 it says: "[Jesus] needed not that any should testify of man: for he knew what was in man." Now the Lord Jesus really puts them on the spot. Is it easier to forgive the sins of this man or to make him arise and walk? Even though they didn't answer, I'm sure they would have said it is just as impossible to do one as the other. Only God could do it. That answer is right and that is why the Lord Jesus told the man to take up his bed and walk.

> But that ye may know that the Son of man hath power on
> earth to forgive sins, (he saith to the sick of the palsy,)
>
> I say unto thee, Arise, and take up thy bed, and go thy
> way into thine house [Mark 2:10,11].

An old Scottish commentator said that the reason He told the
man to take up his bed and walk was because he would not have
a relapse. He wouldn't be back on that bed and he wouldn't be
coming back to the stretcher. He's going to walk from now on.
When our Lord healed, He did a good job of it.

> And immediately he arose, took up the bed, and went
> forth before them all; insomuch that they were all
> amazed, and glorified God, saying, We never saw it on
> this fashion [Mark 2:12].

You see, this is a Gospel of action and here is one of the
miracles of action.

> And he went forth again by the sea side; and all the mul-
> titude resorted unto him, and he taught them.
>
> And as he passed by, he saw Levi the son of Alphaeus
> sitting at the receipt of custom, and said unto him,
> Follow me. And he arose and followed him [Mark
> 2:13,14].

We have continuing action here, although this is not a miracle.
We see a lot of action in this Gospel.

This is the call of Levi, or Matthew. Matthew, by the way,
belonged to the tribe of Levi. Imagine that! He belonged to the
priestly tribe and here he has become a publican, of all things.
And, by the way, this should answer the question about the ten
lost tribes. This is one of the many places where we find an individual who belongs to another tribe besides Judah. When
anyone tries to say there are the ten *lost* tribes today, they must
be on an Easter-egg hunt. Friends, those tribes were not lost.
Here is one of them right here, a man of the tribe of Levi becom-
ing one of the disciples of our Lord. Our Lord is calling him here
in this remarkable incident. You may remember that Matthew
in his Gospel told us nothing about the fact that he gave a great

dinner and invited some of his friends — the only kind of friends he had were sinners, by the way.

And it came to pass, that, as Jesus sat at meat in his house, many publicans and sinners sat also together with Jesus and his disciples: for there were many, and they followed him.

And when the scribes and Pharisees saw him eat with publicans and sinners, they said unto his disciples, How is it that he eateth and drinketh with publicans and sinners? [Mark 2:15,16].

Did you notice that three times here the statement is made that the guests there were publicans and sinners? Apparently there wasn't a good man on the list. None of the elite of the town were there. Notice that the publicans come ahead of the sinners. These were the tax collectors of that day.

When Jesus heard it, he saith unto them, They that are whole have no need of the physician, but they that are sick: I came not to call the righteous, but sinners to repentance [Mark 2:17].

That is a tremendous answer. You don't call for the doctor when everybody is well. It's when you are sick that you want the doctor to come over. The Lord Jesus said that He hadn't come to call the righteous but to call sinners. The reason He said that, actually, was because there were only sinners there. There was only one kind of folk there that day. There was no righteous person there, by any means, but the Pharisees thought *they* were!

And the disciples of John and of the Pharisees used to fast: and they come and say unto him, Why do the disciples of John and of the Pharisees fast, but thy disciples fast not? [Mark 2:18].

They were under the Law, but under the Law there was no instruction given for fasting. God had given seven feasts for His people, not fast days.

And Jesus said unto them, Can the children of the bridechamber fast, while the bridegroom is with them?

as long as they have the bridegroom with them, they cannot fast.

But the days will come, when the bridegroom shall be taken away from them and then shall they fast in those days [Mark 2:19, 20].

What He is saying to them is that it is more important to be related to Him and to have fellowship with Him than it is to fast. It is the same today, friends. It is one thing to be religious and to put up a front, but it's another thing to enjoy fellowship with the Lord Jesus and to love Him.

No man also seweth a piece of new cloth on an old garment; else the new piece that filleth it up taketh away from the old, and the rent is made worse.

And no man putteth new wine into old bottles: else the new wine doth burst the bottles, and the wine is spilled, and the bottles will be marred: but new wine must be put into new bottles [Mark 2:21,22].

The Lord is giving two illustrations about this new life of love and fellowship with Him. He is saying that He did not come to polish up the Law. He didn't come to add to the Mosaic system. He didn't come to add a refinement or a development to it. He came to do something new. He didn't come to patch up an old garment but to give us a new garment.

Under the Law men worked, and their works were like an old moth-eaten garment. Our Lord came to provide a new robe of righteousness that comes down onto a sinner who will trust Christ. This will enable him to stand before Almighty God. This is the glorious, wonderful thing that He is saying here, friends. Our Lord didn't come to extend or project the Law of the Old Testament system or of religion. He came to introduce something new. And that which is new will be the fact that He will die for the sins of the world. New wine goes into new wine skins. A new garment goes onto a new man. That robe of righteousness comes down on one who through faith has become a son of God. This is a tremendous thing!

In the last part of this chapter we come to a Sabbath day in the fields. Then in chapter 3, it begins with the Sabbath day inside the synagogue. We have seen these two incidents in Matthew and in Luke. It is very important because it was on this question of the Sabbath day that He broke with the religious rulers. From this time on, they sought His death.

He claims in this incident that He is the Lord of the Sabbath day. In the synagogue, He does good on the Sabbath day. The question, of course, arises, did He really break the Sabbath in either instance? When He healed the poor man with the withered hand, did He break the Sabbath law? Absolutely He did not. He came to fulfill the Law. But here we find that He is giving an interpretation of this. He reveals that He is the Lord of the Sabbath day, and that doing good was the thing that was all important.

And it came to pass, that he went through the corn fields on the sabbath day; and his disciples began, as they went, to pluck the ears of corn [Mark 2:23].

The "corn" is the Greek *sporima*, meaning sown fields of grain. It may have been barley, or it could have been wheat. The disciples were plucking the grain and eating which the Pharisees interpreted as harvesting grain and thrashing it on the Sabbath. The Law permitted people to pull the grain — we read in Deuteronomy 23:24, 25: "When thou comest into thy neighbour's vineyard, then thou mayest eat grapes thy fill at thine own pleasure; but thou shalt not put any in thy vessel. When thou comest into the standing corn of thy neighbour, then thou mayest pluck the ears with thine hand; but thou shalt not move a sickle unto thy neighbour's standing corn." Actually, they were following the Law. If they had put in a sickle, they would have been harvesting. But the Pharisees had put their own interpretation to it and they would, therefore, interpret the action as breaking the Law.

And the Pharisees said unto him, Behold, why do they on the sabbath day that which is not lawful?

And he said unto them, Have ye never read what David did, when he had need, and was an hungred, he, and they that were with him? [Mark 2:24,25].

He did not insist that they had not broken the Sabbath. Actually, He refused to argue the issue with them. Now He goes into the life of David, their king, and He cited an incident in the life of David where he had definitely broken the Mosaic Law and was justified. You see, the letter of the Law was not to be imposed when it wrought hardship upon one of God's servants who was attempting to serve Him. And that, of course, is the story concerning David, and our Lord uses that illustration.

> **How he went into the house of God in the days of Abiathar the high priest, and did eat the shewbread, which is not lawful to eat but for the priests, and gave also to them which were with him?**
>
> **And he said unto them, The sabbath was made for man, and not man for the sabbath:**
>
> **Therefore the Son of man is Lord also of the sabbath [Mark 2:26-28].**

This is a great principle in respect to the Sabbath day and its meaning. The Law was really made for man and not man for the Sabbath. And, also, here is another great principle and that is, the Lord Jesus is the Lord of the Sabbath. Both those things are very important. By the way, I have a little booklet entitled, *The Sabbath Day or the Lord's Day, Which*? This is a very important question today. Remember that we are not under the old Mosaic system concerning the Sabbath day because it was a part of the covenant between the nation Israel and God (Exodus 31:12-17).

This Sabbath incident in the field and the Sabbath incident which we find at the beginning of chapter 3 should go together; so even though there is a chapter break in the Bible, let us go right on in our study of the incidents that relate to the Sabbath day.

CHAPTER 3

This chapter continues the Sabbath day discussion which led to a final break with the religious rulers.

It is obvious from this chapter that Jesus healed multitudes whose stories could be recorded separately, as the man let down through the roof. Mark impresses us in this chapter, not by placing the microscope down on certain incidents, but by letting us look through the telescope at the multitudes He healed. This raises the question as to the number that Jesus probably dealt with personally. Any attempt to compute the number would be mere speculation. Evidently Mark would have us believe that it was extensive.

> And he entered again into the synagogue; and there was a man there which had a withered hand.
>
> And they watched him, whether he would heal him on the sabbath day; that they might accuse him [Mark 3:1, 2].

The question arises here, was this man, this cripple, planted there purposely? I think the answer is absolutely yes. The other incident was out in the fields, the Sabbath in the corn fields, and that was a *secular* spot. Here it is the Sabbath in the synagogue and this is a *sacred* spot. The Lord Jesus had been healing the multitudes. They knew that if they planted this crippled man right in the way of our Lord, that Jesus would heal him when He came into the synagogue. Actually, what they did was a compliment to the Lord Jesus. They knew He was compassionate. But, of course, they were interested in being able to say that He broke the Sabbath by healing the man on the Sabbath day. So I believe the man was placed there, and we are told that the enemy was there, watching.

Our Lord's enemies are beginning to watch for some little flimsy excuse whereby they might bring a charge against Him. And they are not going to have long to wait, because notice what He did.

**And he saith unto the man which had the withered hand,
Stand forth [Mark 3:3].**

The Lord is going to do something here. I think maybe the
Wycliffe translation is better here: "Rise, come into the midst
and stand there." In other words, He asked this man to come and
stand in the midst because He wants to say something.

**And he saith unto them, Is it lawful to do good on the
sabbath days, or to do evil? to save life, or to kill? But
they held their peace [Mark 3:4].**

They had learned not to answer Him because they always got
into trouble when they did.

**And when he had looked round about on them with
anger, being grieved for the hardness of their hearts, he
saith unto the man, Stretch forth thine hand. And he
stretched it out: and his hand was restored whole as the
other [Mark 3:5].**

Now the Lord Jesus broke through all of this red tape of their
traditions and He got to the heart of God's purpose in giving the
Sabbath day to Israel originally. They wouldn't answer Him
because they knew they would incriminate themselves. Notice
that here the Lord Jesus looks around with anger. You can put it
down in your memory that Jesus could get angry.

Dr. Graham Scroggie notes that the word for "anger" here is in
the aorist tense in the Greek and it carries the sense of momen-
tary anger. The Greek word for "grieve" here is used in the present tense in the sense of a continuing grief. So what we find here
is this: "When He had looked round about on them with anger"
— just a flash of anger, not a grudge or with malice aforethought.
But "being *grieved* for the hardness of their hearts" was something that He carried with Him. He always had that awful grief
because of the hardness of their hearts.

Jesus heals the man. It was the Sabbath but because the Sabbath is made for man and because He is the Lord of the Sabbath,
Jesus healed the man on the Sabbath day. The incident in the
last part of chapter 2 and this incident must be considered
together. These two incidents brought the break with the religious rulers.

And the Pharisees went forth, and straightway took counsel with the Herodians against him, how they might destroy him [Mark 3:6].

Because of these two incidents, both pertaining to the Sabbath day, these bloodhounds of hate got on His trail and they never let up until they folded their arms beneath the cross of Christ. This is the beginning of a plan and plot to put Him to death.

But Jesus withdrew himself with his disciples to the sea: and a great multitude from Galilee followed him, and from Judaea,

And from Jerusalem, and from Idumaea, and from beyond Jordan; and they about Tyre and Sidon, a great multitude, when they had heard what great things he did, came unto him [Mark 3:7, 8].

You will notice people are coming from various areas now and are following Him. Our Lord withdrew tactfully at this time because as He said, "Mine hour is not yet come." (John 2:4). Later on He did move into the face of all the opposition in Jerusalem, but now He withdraws and the crowd follows Him. If you note these places and look them up on a map, you will find they cover that entire area. From all these places folk are coming to hear the Lord Jesus Christ.

Now He is in another danger. This time it is not from the religious rulers because they are afraid of the crowd. He is in danger of being overwhelmed by the mob. You know today that a celebrity has to be protected from the mob — so notice what Jesus does.

And he spake to his disciples, that a small ship should wait on him because of the multitude, lest they should throng him.

For he had healed many; insomuch that they pressed upon him for to touch him, as many as had plagues [Mark 3:9, 10].

The crowds were not only hindering Him but were actually endangering Him. They were pressing in from every side. And we're told that He healed many. You can't reduce "many" to round figures but many means *many*. The Gospels relate to us only a few of the specific examples of His healing of "many." The desperation of the people is also significant. You know, friends, the human family is a needy family. We all belong to this family.

And unclean spirits, when they saw him, fell down before him, and cried, saying, Thou art the Son of God.

And he straitly charged them that they should not make him known [Mark 3:11, 12].

Now we see that the unclean spirits acknowledged Him. We're going to hold that subject for a little later because I want to put an emphasis upon the matter of demon possession at the right time. We are seeing that again today in what is known as Satan worship, and there is a great deal of that going on today. But we see that He did not want the testimony of the underworld. The demons acknowledged who He was, but He didn't want their testimony.

We now begin to see the sovereign purpose of God in choosing and ordaining the twelve apostles.

And he goeth up into a mountain, and calleth unto him whom he would: and they came unto him [Mark 3:13].

This is something I would have you note. He does the choosing here, whether we like it or not. He does the choosing. "Ye have not chosen me, but I have chosen you, and ordained you, that ye should go and bring forth fruit, and that your fruit should remain: that whatsoever ye shall ask of the Father in my name, he may give it you" (John 15:16). It is not irreverent to say that since He chose them and they did not choose Him, He's responsible for them. That's a real comfort to know. God has saved you, begun a good work in you, and He's going to stick right with you, friends. He's going to see you through. That is what this means. And when the Lord Jesus calls, they respond.

And he ordained twelve, that they should be with him, and that he might send them forth to preach,

And to have power to heal sicknesses, and to cast out devils [Mark 3:14, 15].

This is His final call to the apostles. Here is where they actually became apostles, and here is where they are sent out on a ministry set apart for Him. They are also set apart from Him in that He will not go with them physically. Mark does not furnish the details here but in Matthew 10:5-42 there is recorded for us the message and method for them at this particular time.

In verses 16 through 19 the names of the apostles are listed. I would like to run through the list of the twelve:

1. Simon Peter — he is the first in all the lists of the apostles. apostles.
2. James, son of Zebedee, is second here.
3. John is the brother of James.
4. Andrew, brother of Simon Peter. He is customarily listed with his brother.
5. Philip
6. Bartholomew is also called Nathanael.
7. Matthew
8. Thomas
9. James, the less, son of Alphaeus
10. Thaddaeus who is also called Lebbaeus and Jude
11. Simon, the Canaanite
12. Judas Iscariot

I have a book called *Marching through Mark* in which I compare the lists of the apostles as they are given in the four Gospels and in the book of Acts. It is interesting to make this comparison of how they are listed and the different names that are used. These are the men that He chose.

And the multitude cometh together again, so that they could not so much as eat bread.

And when his friends heard *of it*, they went out to lay hold on him: for they said, He is beside himself [Mark 3:20, 21].

Mark will impress us how busy Jesus really was. Note the reaction of His friends. If a man devotes his life to some noble, but earthly cause, he is applauded. The musician, the athlete, the business man, the artist, the statesman who gives himself to his work is recognized for his total devotion. But if a man gives him-

self in total dedication to the cause of God, he is branded as a
fanatic.

> **And the scribes which came down from Jerusalem said,
> He hath Beelzebub, and by the prince of the devils
> casteth he out devils [Mark 3:22].**

Beelzebub was a heathen deity to whom the Jews ascribed
supremacy among evil spirits.

> **And he called them unto him, and said unto them in
> parables, How can Satan cast out Satan?**
>
> **And if a kingdom be divided against itself, that king-
> dom cannot stand.**
>
> **And if a house be divided against itself, that house can-
> not stand.**
>
> **And if Satan rise up against himself, and be divided, he
> cannot stand, but hath an end [Mark 3:23-26].**

What He is saying is simply this: He could not be casting out
demons by the power of the demons for the very simple reason
that then a house would be divided against itself.

> **No man can enter into a strong man's house, and spoil
> his goods, except he will first bind the strong man; and
> then he will spoil his house [Mark 3:27].**

You first have to bind a strong man before you can rob his
house. And that is the truth here. The Lord Jesus is not doing
this by the power of Satan because then Satan would be divided
and would be against himself.

> **Verily I say unto you, All sins shall be forgiven unto the
> sons of men, and blasphemies wherewith soever they
> shall blaspheme:**
>
> **But he that shall blaspheme against the Holy Ghost hath
> never forgiveness, but is in danger of eternal damnation:**
>
> **Because they said, He hath an unclean spirit [Mark 3:28-
> 30].**

That was the unpardonable sin then. It could not be committed today in that way. To begin with, they have Him, the second Person of the Godhead present with them, and they accuse Him of casting out demons by Beelzebub when He was doing it by the power of the Holy Spirit. So they were actually rejecting the works of two Persons of the Godhead, the testimony of the Son and the testimony of the Holy Spirit. They were expressing an attitude of unbelief which was permanent rejection of Christ. They were resisting the Holy Spirit. That was unpardonable.

It is impossible to commit an unpardonable sin today — if by that you mean one can commit a sin today, come under conviction because of it tomorrow, come to God in repentance, and He would not forgive you. You see, Christ died for *all* sin, not just some sin. He didn't die for all sin but *one*, the unpardonable sin. There is no such thing as being able to commit a sin today that He will not forgive. The attitude and state of the unbeliever is unpardonable — not the act. When a man blasphemes with his mouth, that is not the thing that condemns him; it is the attitude of his heart, which is a permanent condition — unless he stops resisting. This is the sin against the Holy Spirit: to resist the convicting work of the Holy Spirit in the heart and life.

There came then his brethren and his mother, and, standing without, sent unto him, calling him.

And the multitude sat about him, and they said unto him, Behold, thy mother and thy brethren without seek for thee.

And he answered them, saying, Who is my mother, or my brethren?

And he looked round about on them which sat about him, and said, Behold my mother and my brethren!

For whosoever shall do the will of God, the same is my brother, and my sister, and mother [Mark 3:31-35].

The half brothers of Jesus, James and Jude, both wrote Epistles, and they never mention that Jesus was their half brother. You see, anyone who is in Christ Jesus is closer to Him than His physical mother and His physical brother were in that day. That is the reason He could look around and say that these are closer kin to Me than even My mother and My brothers. The important thing is to be rightly related to God in Christ Jesus by having received Him as Saviour, which gives us the right of being the sons of God. That is bringing us wonderfully close to Him, my friends.

CHAPTER 4

In this chapter of Mark we find several parables and then the miracle of stopping the storm. This has all been in the Gospel of Matthew except for one particular parable which is given here that is not found in Matthew and it is the only part that makes it different and outstanding, as we shall see. First we find the parable of the sower as a *declaration* and then we have the *exposition* of the parable of the sower. This is followed by other parables and then one miracle.

We said in the beginning of the Gospel of Mark that this is a Gospel of action yet here the emphasis is upon parables with only one miracle. But you will notice that the parables which Mark gives are parables of action. Each one of these parables is really a very moving thing. That's why we titled our booklet on Mark, *Marching Through Mark*. The emphasis is still upon action, even when Mark is giving the parables.

And he began again to teach by the sea side: and there was gathered unto him a great multitude, so that he entered into a ship, and sat in the sea; and the whole multitude was by the sea on the land [Mark 4:1].

Matthew gives us quite an emphasis at this point for he says that Jesus went out of the house as He entered into a ship on the sea. This action as recorded by Matthew is very symbolic. The house generally illustrates the House of Israel, and the seas represent the nations of the Gentiles. His very action is that He turns from His people and He goes to the world. That actually is the background of these parables and they need to be looked at in the context of global situations. I think this is very important for us to see.

These took place, by the way, during the height of His ministry. He was very busy, the pressure was upon Him, and He was physically weary. In fact, He was so tired, as we shall see in this chapter, that He fell asleep in the ship at sea. He was asleep because He was weary.

And he taught them many things by parables, and said unto them in his doctrine [Mark 4:2].

Jesus adopted the use of parables as a way to teach them many things. At this point He is about halfway through His three years of ministry. He had used certain symbolic illustrations before, such as telling the woman at the well about the water of life; He had told His disciples He would make them fishers of men, and that the fields were white unto harvest. Also He had talked about salt, and light, and foundations of rock and sand in the Sermon on the Mount. But these are not parables. Now He has adopted the parabolic method and tells the parable of the sower.

Hearken; Behold, there went out a sower to sow:

And it came to pass, as he sowed, some fell by the way side, and the fowls of the air came and devoured it up.

And some fell on stony ground, where it had not much earth; and immediately it sprang up, because it had no depth of earth:

But when the sun was up, it was scorched; and because it had no root, it withered away.

And some fell among thorns, and the thorns grew up, and choked it, and it yielded no fruit [Mark 4:3-7].

These are the three areas where the seeds fell and they represent the unsaved that do not accept the Gospel. They do not accept the Word of God. Their lives are like the wayside where the birds devour the seed — the devil takes away the Word. Others are like the stony ground where the sun withers it because there is no depth of soil for it. On the thorny ground the thorns choke it.

But then there is the good ground.

And other fell on good ground, and did yield fruit that sprang up and increased; and brought forth, some thirty, and some sixty, and some an hundred [Mark 4:8].

Now here we have only a fourth of it falling on good ground, which represents the ones who are saved, the ones who received the Word. But there are different degrees of fruit-bearing here:

thirty, sixty, and an hundredfold. You remember that the Lord said to His own in that upper-room discourse as He was going out on the way to the Garden of Gethsemane, "I am the genuine vine." Then He told them that He wanted them to bring forth fruit, more fruit, and much fruit. Three degrees of fruit-bearing in those who are His own in that instance, just as we find three degrees in this parable.

And he said unto them, He that hath ears to hear, let him hear [Mark 4:9].

He puts up a danger signal. It's like the "Stop — Look — Listen" sign at a railroad crossing. Even so, it is obvious some missed it because we find in the next verse:

And when he was alone, they that were about him with the twelve asked of him the parable.

And he said unto them, Unto you it is given to know the mystery of the kingdom of God: but unto them that are without, all these things are done in parables:

That seeing they may see, and not perceive; and hearing they may hear, and not understand; lest at any time they should be converted, and their sins should be forgiven them [Mark 4:10-12].

There were obviously some who didn't understand the parable at all. When they ask Him, He answers with these verses that have a certain degree of ambiguity. Let me tell you an explanation that might be helpful. The reason that Jesus resorted to parables at this point to the end of His ministry is arresting. His enemies rejected His teachings and the multitudes had become indifferent to spiritual truths. They were actively interested in His miracles but not the spiritual application. He now resorts to the use of parables to enlist their interest. The antagonistic attitude of His enemies and the lethargy and indifference and incomprehension of the multitudes necessitated a change to the use of parables so that those who hungered and thirsted after righteousness would be filled and those who wanted spiritual truth could have their eyes opened.

We find the same thought in the second chapter of 1 Corinthians, where Paul writes: "But as it is written, Eye hath not seen, nor ear heard, neither have entered into the heart of man, the things which God hath prepared for them that love him. But God hath revealed them unto us by his Spirit: for the Spirit searcheth all things, yea, the deep things of God." Then he goes on in verse 13, "Which things also we speak, not in the words which man's wisdom teacheth, but which the Holy Ghost teacheth; comparing spiritual things with spiritual. But the natural man receiveth not the things of the Spirit of God: for they are foolishness unto him: neither can he know them, because they are spiritually discerned" (1 Corinthians 2:9,10,13,14).

This is a great principle that Paul put down, and it is still applicable today. We can use every means to try to get people to understand spiritual truth, but they must want to understand them before these things can be made real to them. I would like to make this statement: If a person's heart and eyes are open and he wants to know, then the Spirit of God is going to bring in the great truth to his heart. He will make these things quite real and living for that person.

We sometimes use the expression — I know I say it rather carelessly — that you'll be lost if you do not accept Christ as your Saviour. That is not really the truth, friends. The truth is that you are *already* lost. The point that should be accurately stated is that you will continue to be lost if you do not receive Christ as your Saviour. You're not on trial, my friend. If you are a lost person, you are *lost*. Now it is your reaction and reception to the Word of God that is going to determine whether you will be saved or not. Will you trust Christ? Will you accept Him as your Saviour?

Somebody may say that this is beginning to move into a philosophical realm and this is not reality. This is asking a person to do something that is rather spooky, rather superstitious. I don't think it is at all, my friend. Let me illustrate it.

Mrs. McGee and I were down in Florida and found that we had bought tickets from an airline that was out on strike. We had to go back to Los Angeles on another airline, but we could use our original tickets. When I called the girl at the airport, she was able to confirm the fact that we had tickets with the airline that was on strike, and she assured us our tickets were good, our plane would leave the next morning at a certain time, and we should get to the airport about thirty minutes ahead of that time. You know, friends, I have never met this girl — not even to this good day — but I believed her. Mrs. McGee and I were there at the airport the next morning. Our tickets were good. The plane was there and we boarded it. We believed every bit of the information about that plane, and don't try to tell me that plane was not a reality. In just such a way God has given His Word. He asks you to trust Christ.

God's Word is the seed that falls. What kind of soil are you today? Are you the one with the thorns so the seed falls by the wayside or on thorny ground? Or does God's Word fall on good ground? That is the important thing. All of us are lost, and it is our *reception* to the Word of God that determines whether we are saved or whether we remain lost.

Now He gives the exposition of the parable up through verse 20.

And he said unto them, Know ye not this parable? and how then will ye know all parables?

The sower soweth the word.

And these are they by the way side, where the word is sown; but when they have heard, Satan cometh immediately, and taketh away the word that was sown in their hearts.

And these are they likewise which are sown on stony ground; who, when they have heard the word, immediately receive it with gladness;

And have no root in themselves, and so endure but for a time: afterward, when affliction or persecution ariseth for the word's sake, immediately they are offended.

And these are they which are sown among thorns; such as hear the word,

And the cares of this world, and the deceitfulness of riches, and the lusts of other things entering in, choke the word, and it becometh unfruitful.

And these are they which are sown on good ground; such as hear the word, and receive it, and bring forth fruit, some thirtyfold, some sixty, and some an hundred [Mark 4:13-20].

I'll go over it quickly. The sower is the Son of Man and the seed is the Word of God. The birds by the wayside are Satan. The stony-ground hearers are those who let affliction and persecution turn them from God. That is the flesh, and many people today are letting the flesh keep them from God. Then there are the thorny-ground hearers, those who let the cares of the world distract them. That is the world today. So many people today are letting the world shut them out from God. Then the good-ground hearers are those who are converted genuinely by the Word of God. They bring forth only percentages of fruit and only one third of these bring forth an hundredfold. So we see that we have here a parable with real action.

And he said unto them, Is a candle brought to be put under a bushel, or under a bed? and not to be set on a candlestick?

For there is nothing hid, which shall not be manifested; neither was any thing kept secret, but that it should come abroad [Mark 4:21, 22].

What we have here is a parable of the candle and its action. Light creates responsibility. A man who receives the truth must act. We are held responsible to the degree to which we have had light given us. The light is shining, and your response to the light is all important. The point is, you and I were in darkness until the light of the Gospel got through to us. We get the impression that man is a sinner because of his weakness or because of his ignorance. But Paul says very candidly (in Romans 1) that men, when they knew God, glorified Him not as God. Man is a *willful* sinner. That's the kind of sinners all of us are, and the light that comes in will create a responsibility. We are lost, and if we do not accept the Light, if we do not accept Him, we remain lost.

If any man have ears to hear, let him hear [Mark 4:23].

This is action. God demands this action. Faith is action. Faith is acting upon what God has said. How important that is today.

I come back to the illustration of our plane trip. You must act on the fact that you have a ticket. You must believe and trust that there is a plane, and that it is going to carry you right to the place you wish to go. But just sitting there in the airport depot *believing it* won't get you there. You must believe it enough to board the plane. That is what it means to believe.

And he said, So is the kingdom of God, as if a man should cast seed into the ground;

And should sleep, and rise night and day, and the seed should spring and grow up, he knoweth not how.

For the earth bringeth forth fruit of herself; first the blade, then the ear, after that the full corn in the ear.

But when the fruit is brought forth, immediately he putteth in the sickle, because the harvest is come [Mark 4:26-29].

Here is an unusual parable that our Lord gave and only Mark records it. It is another parable of action. It is about the "Kingdom of God." Remember that I said the Kingdom of God and the Kingdom of Heaven are two terms that are used. Actually, here they are synonymous but the Kingdom of God is not identical with the Kingdom of Heaven. The Kingdom of God is the larger term including the whole universe; the Kingdom of Heaven is God's rule over the earth, which is, of course, in the Kingdom of God. For instance, the state of California is in the United States, but it is not the United States. It is *in* it. So when I am in California, I am also in the United States.

Our Lord talks about the growing of the seed here. Even today we still don't know too much about the growing of a seed into a plant, then producing fruit. It is a mystery to this day. This is another parable of power and action. The old bromide is true:"Great oaks from little acorns grow." After all of the years of scientific progress, there is not much more men can add to this. The label of osmosis adds little to our understanding, although the reservoir of knowledge has been increased.

During the month of March I travelled by train from Atlanta, Georgia, to Los Angeles, California. Spring had already come to the southern section of our country. Trees were budding, flowers were blooming — the azaleas in Mississippi were gorgeous, and the farmers everywhere were plowing and planting. No one could tell just what was happening, but everyone was reacting to it and accepting it with full enjoyment and happy anticipation of the future harvest. Tremendous power was being released in nature as nitrogen took on the garment of green. If God let it go at once it would make a hydrogen bomb sound like a Chinese firecracker.

This parable illustrates the power of the Word of God working in our hearts and lives. What a marvelous parable it is.

Now we have the third parable about seed in this chapter.

> And he said, Whereunto shall we liken the kingdom of God? or with what comparison shall we compare it?
>
> It is like a grain of mustard seed, which, when it is sown in the earth, is less than all the seeds that be in the earth:
>
> But when it is sown, it groweth up, and becometh greater than all herbs, and shooteth out great branches; so that the fowls of the air may lodge under the shadow of it.
>
> And with many such parables spake he the word unto them, as they were able to hear it.
>
> But without a parable spake he not unto them: and when they were alone, he expounded all things to his disciples [Mark 4:30-34].

Mustard is not food but is a condiment. And the growth of a mustard seed into a tree is unnatural. This pictures the outward growth of Christendom into great organizations, big churches, large programs, all produced by human energy, and not by the Holy Spirit. The birds in the branches are not even good. They represent Satan.

Now we find here that when our Lord leaves off teaching, they go out into the sea. He wants a rest because He's tired. He goes to sleep. And then we find this miracle of Him quieting the sea.

> And the same day, when the even was come, he saith unto them, Let us pass over unto the other side.

And when they had sent away the multitude, they took him even as he was in the ship. And there were also with him other little ships.

And there arose a great storm of wind, and the waves beat into the ship, so that it was now full.

And he was in the hinder part of the ship, asleep on a pillow: and they awake him, and say unto him, Master, carest thou not that we perish?

And he arose, and rebuked the wind, and said unto the sea, Peace, be still. And the wind ceased, and there was a great calm.

And he said unto them, Why are ye so fearful? how is it that ye have no faith?

And they feared exceedingly, and said one to another, What manner of man is this, that even the wind and the sea obey him? [Mark 4:35-41].

Do you know what made them fear? It was not so much the fact that He quieted the storm, but that it responded immediately. It just leveled out; there was a sudden calm. This miracle was so great that it made these men afraid.

What a wonderful lesson we learn here. He puts us into the storms of life in order that we might grow closer to Him and that we might know Him better.

> Jesus, Saviour, pilot me
> Over life's tempestuous sea.
> Unknown waves before me roll.
> Hiding rocks and treacherous shoal.
> Chart and compass come from Thee.
> Jesus, Saviour, pilot me.

CHAPTER 5

We come now to one of the most important chapters in the Gospel of Mark. I'm sure some of you are smiling now, because I think I say that about every chapter we study. Well, every chapter *is* the most important chapter when you are studying it! But this one is important because the Gospel of Mark is a Gospel of action. There are more of the miracles given in this Gospel than in any other, and in this chapter there are three outstanding miracles related. They could be performed only by the hand of Omnipotence. That is why I think this is a remarkable chapter.

Let me say just a word today about demon possession. We promised it on several occasions in Matthew, and when we began Mark we said that we'd have something a little more detailed to say concerning it. This is the place.

And they came over unto the other side of the sea, into the country of the Gadarenes [Mark 5:1].

Our Lord had taught on the other side and had given them parables. He was weary and so had crossed the sea. The Gadarenes were the inhabitants of Gadara, and this is the land that was given to the tribe of Gad on the east side of the Jordan River. Remember, Gad chose the wrong side of Jordan. They were the ones that stayed on the east side, and now we find them in the pig business. You see, when you start away from God, you just keep going away from Him.

And when he was come out of the ship, immediately there met him out of the tombs a man with an unclean spirit [Mark 5:2].

He's "a man," a human being. Note that first of all and write it down. He is in a desperate condition but he is still a man. That is what the Lord Jesus saw — a man. In spite of his condition, Jesus saw the man. His conduct suggests that the man was a maniac. Notice what it says about him.

Who had his dwelling among the tombs; and no man could bind him, no, not with chains:

Because that he had been often bound with fetters and chains, and the chains had been plucked asunder by him, and the fetters broken in pieces: neither could any man tame him.

And always, night and day, he was in the mountains, and in the tombs, crying, and cutting himself with stones [Mark 5:3-5].

This is a desperate case of a man possessed with this unclean spirit. He dwelt, which means he settled down, among the tombs. This is where he lived; this was his ghetto. The tombs were unclean places. The dead were there, and sometimes the bodies were exposed. He no longer enjoyed the society of normal men but he lived among the dead. We find from Matthew that there was another man, but Mark and Luke center on this one. We gather that the other man was no companion to this man, nor, of course, were the dead any company to him. He was alone. Yet we are told that he possessed superhuman power; so they could not bind him. Just because a man demonstrates power which is supernatural does not prove that God gave it to him. This case is a typical example. He was a wild man; so no one could confine him. He was miserable. He suffered great physical harm which he inflicted on himself. He's a creature of pathos and pity, and on the human plane he is a hopeless case. He's inarticulate and just crying out. What an awful condition! And all due to demon possession!

But when he saw Jesus afar off, he ran and worshipped him.

And cried with a loud voice, and said, What have I to do with thee, Jesus, thou Son of the most high God? I adjure thee by God, that thou torment me not.

For he said unto him, Come out of the man, thou unclean spirit [Mark 5:6-8].

It was the man who worshipped Him, not the demon. He was afraid of Jesus. He suffered, I think you would call it, spiritual schizophrenia, a split personality. Sometimes it is the man and sometimes it is the demon speaking. In verse 7 it literally says, "What is there to thee and me?" That is, "What have we in common?" This poor man — possessed by demons!

And he asked him, What is thy name? And he answered, saying, My name is Legion: for we are many [Mark 5:9].

The answer of this man is baffling but it's not bad grammar. He says, "My name is . . ." indicating that the man was trying to speak, but then the demons take over and they say, "We are many."

And he besought him much that he would not send them away out of the country.

Now there was there nigh unto the mountains a great herd of swine feeding.

And all the devils besought him, saying, Send us into the swine, that we may enter into them.

And forthwith Jesus gave them leave. And the unclean spirits went out, and entered into the swine: and the herd ran violently down a steep place into the sea, (they were about two thousand;) and were choked in the sea [Mark 5:10-13].

There is a tremendous occurrence presented to us here. The demons made a very peculiar request. They preferred swine to the abyss. The permission of Jesus here has been severely criticized by men who are liberal in their theology. Their objection has been that He would not destroy the swine, as the "gentle Jesus" wouldn't do things like that. That's nonsense, of course. I was having breakfast in Chicago with a man who had gone into liberalism. I had known him in school, and he had been sound then, but the way he was talking about Jesus and describing Him, was totally fictitious. And he used this illustration, saying he didn't believe Jesus would destroy swine because that was such a terrible thing. Well, to begin with, these people shouldn't have been in the pig business. The Mosaic Law forbade it. And then I reminded this fellow that the two thousand pigs destroyed here was insignificant compared to the pigs that were destroyed in the Flood at the time of Noah. And the third interesting thing was that as we were having breakfast together, he was eating bacon. Oh, my! I said to him, "I wish the little piggie that you are eating this morning were here to tell you what he thinks of you, for you weep like the walrus and the carpenter." (You remember, they just kept on eating the oysters but they wept because there was a lot of sand, not because they were eating the oysters. They wept for the wrong thing.) Well, I think we have a lot of that type of thinking about us today.

Now let me come back and say some things about this matter of demon possession:

1. Not only Mark but all of the Scriptures bear definite witness to the reality of demons. For those who accept the authority of Scripture, there must be an acceptance of the reality of demons.

2. They were especially evident during the ministry of Jesus, but, of course, were not confined to that period. By the way, we're living in a day right now where we see a resurgence and a manifestation of demonism again. Many illustrations of this could be given.

3. For some strange reason they seek to indwell mankind. They seek to manifest their evil nature through human beings. They are extremely restless. This description is clear. "When the unclean spirit is gone out of a man, he walketh through dry places, seeking rest; and finding none, he saith, I will return unto my house whence I came out" (Luke 11:24). Is this not the characteristic of all evil, even evil men? There is the restlessness of seeking expression of the evil nature.

Good spirits never seek to take possession of men. The Holy Spirit is the one exception, and He only indwells believers. But as truly as He indwells believers so demons can possess the unsaved. Demons cannot possess the saved. We are told that greater is He that is in us (the Holy Spirit) than he that is in the world (Satan) (I John 4:4). Therefore, a child of God cannot be demon possessed.

4. In this incident the demons would rather go into a herd of swine than the abyss. That is interesting to note.

5. They should be called demons and not devils. There is only one devil. Our translation is faulty here. They are called "unclean spirits" because of their nature.

6. Scripture does not give us the origin of them. Anything I would say today would be highly speculative.

7. There seems to be many of them.

8. They are under the control of Satan. Now I said I would not speculate, but here I go. I'm of the opinion that when Satan fell, these were the angels that followed him. Now having said that, let's not say any more.

9. Their purpose is the final undoing of man. They are certainly working on Satan's program.

10. There are present-day examples of demon possession. We have Satan worship right in our own neighborhoods, and there are a lot of college students and professors who are engaged in it. They say they find reality in it. I think they do, by the way. I think that Satan is prepared to give reality to those who worship him. The all-important question is: what kind of reality do they find?

11. The Lord Jesus Christ has power over demons. That, I think, is the great lesson for us to learn.

There is no reason for any believer to be afraid of demons or to adopt some superstition or spooky notion concerning them. If you feel that you are bothered with them, then just ask the Lord Jesus to deliver you. They have been cast out in His name, and it is a lack of faith in the Lord Jesus to walk in fear of them today. If you feel that they can control you in any way, or possess you, or direct you, then you need counselling. Remember that the Lord Jesus Christ has power over demons.

There is a very pertinent poem written by Joseph Odell about this incident. You know that the people of Gadara came and asked the Lord Jesus to leave their coast. The reason was that they would rather have swine than have *Him*. That's a rather heart-searching question for the present day because there are a lot of people who would rather have other things — that are just as bad as pigs — than to have Christ.

> Rabbi, begone! Thy powers
> Bring loss to us and ours.
> Our ways are not as Thine,

Thou lovest men, we — swine.
Oh, get Thee hence, Omnipotence!
And take this fool of Thine!
His soul? What care we for his soul?
What good to us that Thou has made him whole?
Since we have lost our swine.
And Christ went sadly,
He had wrought for them a sign
Of love and hope and tenderness divine —
They wanted swine.

Christ stands without your door and gently knocks,
But if your gold or swine the entrance blocks,
He forces no man's hold — he will depart
And leave you to the treasures of your heart.
No cumbered chamber will the Master share,
But one swept bare
By cleansing fires, then plenished fresh and fair
With meekness and humility and prayer.
There he will come, yet coming, even there
He stands and waits and will no entrance win
Until the latch be lifted from within.

— Joseph H. Odell

The next miracle is closely connected with the miracle of the raising of the daughter of Jairus.

And when Jesus was passed over again by ship unto the other side, much people gathered unto him: and he was nigh unto the sea.

And behold, there cometh one of the rulers of the synagogue, Jairus by name; and when he saw him, he fell at his feet,

And besought him greatly, saying, My little daughter lieth at the point of death: I pray thee, come and lay thy hands on her, that she may be healed; and she shall live.

And Jesus went with him; and much people followed him, and thronged him.

And a certain woman, which had an issue of blood twelve years,

And had suffered many things of many physicians, and had spent all that she had, and was nothing bettered, but rather grew worse,

When she had heard of Jesus, came in the press behind, and touched his garment.

For she said, If I may touch but his clothes, I shall be whole [Mark 5:21-28].

Now Jesus has returned again to His land. In telling this incident, it is interesting that Luke, who was a physician, said she couldn't be healed. Mark says that she had suffered many things of the physicians, and she had spent all that she had. So we see that this matter of medical expense being so great today is not new at all.

And straightway the fountain of her blood was dried up; and she felt in her body that she was healed of that plague.

And Jesus, immediately knowing in himself that virtue had gone out of him, turned him about in the press, and said, Who touched my clothes?

And his disciples said unto him, Thou seest the multitude thronging thee, and sayest thou, Who touched me? [Mark 5:29-31].

The disciples thought it was a very peculiar question since the whole crowd was pressing in on Him. But only one touched Him in faith for healing!

The situation is the same today. I think we have a lot of folk around who use the name of Jesus freely. They are running around saying that it is Jesus this, and Jesus that, and people think they certainly know Him. Surely they know Him, but they have touched Him as the crowd touched Him — not like this woman touched Him, for she touched Him in faith for healing.

And he looked round about to see her that had done this thing.

> But the woman fearing and trembling, knowing what was done in her, came and fell down before him, and told him all the truth.
>
> And he said unto her, Daughter, thy faith hath made thee whole; go in peace, and be whole of thy plague [Mark 5:32-34].

She had been in this condition for twelve years. Did you notice that the little girl was twelve years old? Twelve years of suffering coming to an end and twelve years light entering into darkness, the darkness of death. The father who had come, when he saw our Lord talking to this woman and dealing with her, I'm sure thought, *Oh, why doesn't He hurry. Doesn't He know that my little girl is so sick at home that she'll die unless He moves?* Our Lord purposely did not move. He healed this woman, and while He is dealing with her, one comes with a message. He whispers to him.

> While he yet spake, there came from the ruler of the synagogue's house certain which said, Thy daughter is dead: why troublest thou the Master any further?
>
> As soon as Jesus heard the word that was spoken, he saith unto the ruler of the synagogue, Be not afraid, only believe.
>
> And he suffered no man to follow him, save Peter, and James, and John the brother of James.
>
> And he cometh to the house of the ruler of the synagogue, and seeth the tumult, and them that wept and wailed greatly.
>
> And when he was come in, he saith unto them, Why make ye this ado, and weep? the damsel is not dead, but sleepeth.
>
> And they laughed him to scorn. But when he had put them all out, he taketh the father and the mother of the damsel, and them that were with him, and entereth in where the damsel was lying [Mark 5:35-40].

So Jesus goes to the home, and puts out those who don't

believe. When they were out, He goes in and the record tells us:

And he took the damsel by the hand, and said unto her, Talitha cumi; which is, being interpreted, Damsel, I say unto thee, arise [Mark 5:41].

"Talitha cumi" was an expression of the Aramaic that the little girl would have understood. It was her native tongue and I think it could be translated "Little lamb, wake up!" That's what He said to her and that is a sweet, lovely thing. We find that our Lord raised a little girl, He raised a man in the vigor of young manhood (the widow's son at Nain), and then probably a mature man or even a senior citizen, Lazarus. He raised them all the same way. He spoke to them!

I think this little girl represents the little folks, those little ones before they reach the age of accountability. And He said to her in this lovely way, "Little lamb, wake up." I know right now I'm speaking to a lot of folk who have lost little ones. When we lost our first little one, what a sad thing it was for us. It's wonderful for me to know that although she has been in His presence for many years, one of these days He's going to speak those words again, "Little lamb, wake up!" He'll be talking to my little lamb and to your little lamb. Then that little form that we laid away will be raised from the grave, the spirit joined to the glorified body, and we will again have our little ones some day. What a wonderful, beautiful thing this is. It is a demonstration of His power.

And straightway the damsel arose, and walked; for she was of the age of twelve years. And they were astonished with a great astonishment.

And he charged them straitly that no man should know it; and commanded that something should be given her to eat [Mark 5:42,43].

Isn't that practical? If a twelve-year-old girl, or boy for that matter, were waked up from sleep and were made well, what would they want? Food, of course. So He told them to feed the little one. How practical this is and how wonderful it is.

These are the three great miracles that to my judgment demonstrate the great message of the Gospel of Mark. He is

God's Servant with God's power. He is a Man of action and He has come not to be ministered to but to minister and to give His life a ransom for many. Here we see Him in this chapter doing three wonderful miracles. He casts out demons from the man in Gadara. He heals the woman with an issue of blood. He raises this little twelve-year-old daughter of Jairus.

CHAPTER 6

This is the second longest chapter in the Gospel of Mark. Mark follows his usual style of presenting the action in the ministry of Jesus with machine gun like rapidity, but in the first twenty-nine verses there is a lull in the intense activity. Jesus returns to Nazareth. He sends out the Twelve to preach and they report back to Him. Then He feeds the 5,000, walks on the water, and heals in the land of Gennesaret. The chapter closes with the ministry of Jesus around the Sea of Galilee in the locality of the western shore. Jesus is tremendously popular at this time. It is the peak of His ministry.

And he went out from thence, and came into his own country; and his disciples follow him.

And when the sabbath day was come, he began to teach in the synagogue: and many hearing him were astonished, saying, From whence hath this man these things? and what wisdom is this which is given unto him, that even such mighty works are wrought by his hands?

Is not this the carpenter, the son of Mary, the brother of James, and Joses, and of Juda, and Simon? and are not his sisters here with us? And they were offended at him [Mark 6:1-3].

When this incident has been compared with the fourth chapter of Luke, the critics say that it reveals a contradiction in the Bible. They say the two accounts conflict one with the other. The fact of the matter is that we have the record of two visits that our Lord made to His home town of Nazareth. I think He probably made other visits to Nazareth, but these are the two that are recorded. Luke 4 relates the first visit and He went there alone. He performed no miracle and He left suddenly when they tried to kill Him. On the second visit, which is recorded here in Mark 6, we find His disciples are with Him, that He healed "a few sick folk," and that He remained in this area. This is based on information from Matthew 13:53-58 as well as this chapter of Mark 6. On both occasions He entered the synagogue and taught, and on both occasions He was rejected by His fellow townspeople. So this is not a conflict, but rather two records of two visits that He made to His hometown. The first time He left, He went down to Capernaum and made that His headquarters. But He returned because He wanted to reach His hometown people.

In the first verse when it says "his own country," it literally means His fatherland. It was the custom of our Lord to go to the synagogue on the Sabbath day wherever He was. I think He felt the need to worship God in this way, and also, it was the place to reach the people of that day. His teaching amazed those who had known Him. His words, His works, His wonders all occasioned a consternation on the part of His fellow citizens, which prompted their questions. They actually did not believe that Nazareth could produce anyone like Jesus. They were looking at themselves, of course, and judging Nazareth by themselves. Nazareth hadn't done too well by them — so they figured there couldn't be One like the Lord Jesus. They had no faith in One of their own and they had no faith in themselves.

This passage also reveals that Mary had other children. These were half brothers and sisters of Jesus. I think the Jude that is mentioned here is the author of the Epistle of Jude. And they were *scandalized* because of Him. They thought that they knew Him, which was, of course, their stumbling stone. I think there is a danger in getting familiar with Jesus. He is One that we don't get familiar with at all. That was their problem. They thought they knew Him, but they did not. They had seen Him as a boy grow up in the town.

> **But Jesus said unto them, A prophet is not without honour, but in his own country, and among his own kin, and in his own house [Mark 6:4].**

I think the common colloquialism of the day is apropos here, "An expert is an ordinary fellow from another town." We think that whoever comes from afar knows more than our crowd knows. I guess maybe that is the reason some of us go up and down and through the country ministering elsewhere. Sometimes many of us are more effective away from home than we are at home.

> **And he could there do no mighty work, save that he laid his hands upon a few sick folk, and healed them.**

And he marvelled because of their unbelief. And he went round about the villages, teaching [Mark 6:5,6].

You see that He did not leave this area at this time but stayed in the vicinity. The first time He had been practically run out of town and had gone down to Capernaum to make His headquarters there. This is a remarkable passage because it tells us He couldn't perform any mighty works there because of their unbelief.

The only limitation to omnipotence is unbelief. Faith is the one requirement to release the power of God in salvation. In the great chapter of Isaiah 53 that reveals God's so great salvation, the prophet opens the chapter with: "Who hath believed our report? and to whom is the arm of the Lord revealed?" (Isaiah 53:1). Who will believe it? My friend, unbelief shuts off Omnipotence. Unbelief insulates and isolates the power of God. It still does that today!

He marvelled at their unbelief (verse 6). This is not the only time we notice that He marvels. In Matthew 8:10 — "When Jesus heard it, he marvelled, and said to them that followed, Verily I say unto you, I have not found so great faith, no, not in Israel" — He was speaking of the faith of the centurion.

Now we notice that He went round about the villages teaching. This is a wonderful lesson for Christian workers. There are certain men in God's work who do not want to go to a small place to minister. I've actually been criticized by some ministers and Christian workers for going to certain small churches instead of going to the large church. My feeling is that our Lord set us a tremendous example here when it says that He went about their villages. Imagine, friends, the Lord of Glory, the Son of God here on this earth ministering in little villages. He could have sent a telegram over to Rome and hired the Colosseum for a big meeting! Today we have men who are suffering from megalomania. They feel they have to have a big crowd. All of us need to learn a lesson from Jesus.

There is a story about Dr. C. I. Scofield, the man who was responsible for *The Scofield Reference Bible*. He had been invited to speak in a church in North Carolina. It was a rainy night; so about twenty-five people came to the meeting. The young preacher leaned over and apologized to Dr. Scofield for the small number who had come to hear his preaching and teaching. Dr. Scofield replied, "Young man, my Lord had only twelve men in His school and in His congregation most of the time. If He had only twelve, who is C. I. Scofield to be concerned about a big crowd?"

> **And he called unto him the twelve, and began to send them forth by two and two; and gave them power over unclean spirits [Mark 6:7].**

He is now sending out His disciples, and He sends them with the message of repentance which is the same message He has been preaching. He sends them two by two. It's interesting that neither Matthew nor Luke told us that when they record this incident. He gave them power over unclean spirits which seems to be the very highest power they could exercise.

> **And commanded them that they should take nothing for their journey, save a staff only; no scrip, no bread, no money in their purse;**
>
> **But be shod with sandals; and not put on two coats [Mark 6:8-9].**

Why such a command? Well, they were to travel light. This is to indicate the urgency and the lateness of the hour, and the importance of their mission, and their total dependence upon God. Later on, we shall find that they were told to take these things because they were going on a longer journey. Matthew makes it clear that this time they were to go only to the lost sheep of the House of Israel, and they were to accept the hospitality that was offered to them.

> **And he said unto them, In what place soever ye enter into an house, there abide till ye depart from that place.**
>
> **And whosoever shall not receive you, nor hear you, when ye depart thence, shake off the dust under your feet for a testimony against them. Verily I say unto you, It shall be more tolerable for Sodom and Gomorrha in the day of judgment, than for that city [Mark 6:10, 11].**

This is a serious and a solemn trip they are to take. Light

creates responsibility. To reject the grace of God invited His judgment. The same is still true today.

And they went out, and preached that men should repent.

And they cast out many devils, and anointed with oil many that were sick, and healed them [Mark 6:12,13].

They preached a message of repentance, and the miracles authenticated their message. This commission was limited to the lost sheep of the House of Israel. It is not the pattern for today. Repentance is part of the Gospel message, however; it is contained in the command to *believe*.

The record of this incident is longer in the Gospel of Matthew and we go into more detail in our study of it in that Gospel. The fame of Jesus had spread throughout that area. Not only the common people but even Herod on the throne had heard of Jesus. Now we find this strange reaction on the part of King Herod. The murder of John the Baptist had taken place sometime before. I think it is recorded here to explain Herod's strange and superstitious reaction.

And king Herod heard of him; (for his name was spread abroad:) and he said, That John the Baptist was risen from the dead, and therefore mighty works do shew forth themselves in him.

Others said, That it is Elias. And others said, That it is a prophet, or as one of the prophets [Mark 6:14,15].

We can see that this man Herod is very superstitious. But there was a great deal of mingled reaction among the people about the Lord Jesus as to who He was. There is that same reaction today, by the way. We find that different people have different viewpoints and different explanations of the Person, the presence, and the power of the Lord Jesus. So there was this confusion, and Herod was definitely afraid.

But when Herod heard thereof, he said, It is John, whom I beheaded: he is risen from the dead [Mark 6:16].

Herod was afraid.

> For Herod himself had sent forth and laid hold upon John, and bound him in prison for Herodias' sake, his brother Philip's wife: for he had married her.
>
> For John had said unto Herod, It is not lawful for thee to have thy brother's wife [Mark 6:17,18].

The murder of John had taken place previous to this point in the ministry of Jesus. Notice that John boldly denounced sin in high places. He had denounced Herod for taking Herodias, his brother's wife. This enraged her and caused her to plot John's death.

> Therefore Herodias had a quarrel against him, and would have killed him; but she could not:
>
> For Herod feared John, knowing that he was a just man and an holy, and observed him; and when he heard him, he did many things, and heard him gladly [Mark 6:19,20].

Did Herodias keep Herod from turning to God?

> And when a convenient day was come, that Herod on his birthday made a supper to his lords, high captains, and chief estates of Galilee;
>
> And when the daughter of the said Herodias came in, and danced, and pleased Herod and them that sat with him, the king said unto the damsel, Ask of me whatsoever thou wilt, and I will give it thee [Mark 6:21,22].

Herodias had asked her daughter to dance before him because she knew what a lecherous, lustful old man he was. He gave the daughter a blank check and she could ask anything she wanted.

> And he sware unto her, Whatsoever thou shalt ask of me, I will give it thee, unto the half of my kingdom.
>
> And she went forth, and said unto her mother, What shall I ask? And she said, The head of John the Baptist [Mark 6:23,24].

The mother was prepared for this. The brutality of this woman boggles the mind.

And she came in straightway with haste unto the king, and asked, saying, I will that thou give me by and by in a charger the head of John the Baptist.

And the king was exceeding sorry; yet for his oath's sake, and for their sakes which sat with him, he would not reject her [Mark 6:25,26].

Another weakness of Herod is revealed here. He is afraid of what his friends might think and say. He had a false sense of values about an oath.

And immediately the king sent an executioner, and commanded his head to be brought: and he went and beheaded him in the prison,

And brought his head in a charger, and gave it to the damsel: and the damsel gave it to her mother [Mark 6:27,28].

This was cold-blooded murder!

And when his disciples heard of it, they came and took up his corpse, and laid it in a tomb [Mark 6:29].

The disciples of John took up the decapitated body of John, and tenderly buried it.

Mark now returns the narrative to the ministry of Jesus. The apostles make their first report. Note the absence of details.

And the apostles gathered themselves together unto Jesus, and told him all things, both what they had done, and what they had taught.

And he said unto them, Come ye yourselves apart into a desert place, and rest a while: for there were many coming and going, and they had no leisure so much as to eat [Mark 6:30,31].

It is impossible for us to understand how really busy the Lord Jesus was and how great the demands were upon Him. He had to withdraw to an uninhabited place in an attempt to rest and let His apostles rest.

And they departed into a desert place by ship privately.

And the people saw them departing, and many knew him, and ran afoot thither out of all cities, and outwent them, and came together unto him.

And Jesus, when he came out, saw much people, and was moved with compassion toward them, because they were as sheep not having a shepherd: and he began to teach them many things. [Mark 6:32-34].

It was futile to try to find a place to be alone. The crowd followed around the shore of the Sea of Galilee, and they were there to meet Jesus and the disciples when they landed. The reaction of Jesus was one of complete sympathy. All people are sheep to Him. He alone is the true Shepherd. This is the reason He fed them. He first met their spiritual needs by teaching them. Then He met their physical needs by feeding them.

And when the day was now far spent, his disciples came unto him, and said, This is a desert place, and now the time *is* far passed:

Send them away, that they may go into the country round about, and into the villages, and buy themselves bread: for they have nothing to eat.

He answered and said unto them, Give ye them to eat. And they say unto him, Shall we go and buy two hundred pennyworth of bread, and give them to eat? [Mark 6:35-37].

He commands them to do an impossible task. They must learn, as we must learn, that He always commands the impossible. The reason is obvious. He intends to do the work.

He saith unto them, How many loaves have ye? go and see. And when they knew, they say, Five, and two fishes.

And he commanded them to make all sit down by companies upon the green grass.

And they sat down in ranks, by hundreds, and by fifties.

And when he had taken the five loaves and the two

fishes, he looked up to heaven, and blessed, and brake the loaves, and gave *them* to his disciples to set before them; and the two fishes divided he among them all.

And they did all eat, and were filled.

And they took up twelve baskets full of the fragments, and of the fishes.

And they that did eat of the loaves were about five thousand men [Mark 6:38-44].

This is a miracle. The Creator who made the fish at the beginning and caused the grain to multiply in the field, now by His fiat word creates food for the crowd. This may have been the first time many in this crowd ever were filled.

And straightway he constrained his disciples to get into the ship, and to go to the other side before unto Beth-sa-i-da, while he sent away the people [Mark 6:45].

There is an urgency expressed in the two words "straightway" and "constrained." The explanation is found in John 6:15. Jesus perceived that they would try by force to make Him a king.

And when he had sent them away, he departed into a mountain to pray.

And when even was come, the ship was in the midst of the sea, and he alone on the land.

And he saw them toiling in rowing; for the wind was contrary unto them; and about the fourth watch of the night he cometh unto them, walking upon the sea, and would have passed by them.

But when they saw him walking upon the sea, they supposed it had been a spirit, and cried out.

For they all saw him, and were troubled. And immediately he talked with them, and saith unto them, Be of good cheer: it is I; be not afraid.

And he went up unto them into the ship; and the wind ceased: and they were sore amazed in themselves beyond measure, and wondered.

For they considered not the miracle of the loaves: for their heart was hardened [Mark 6:46-52].

Note that here we find no record of Simon Peter coming to Him walking on the water. After all, Mark got his information on the human plane from Simon Peter, and Peter just left out his part of the story. It is Matthew who gives us that detail.

I do want to call your attention to verse 48 where it says, "And he saw them toiling in rowing . . ." Those men were in the boat that night and they were mingling their sweat with the waves whose water was breaking over their little boat. They were straining at the oars and they actually thought they were going down. But He saw them toiling and rowing. I love that! I don't know where you are today or what position you are in. You may be in a hard spot right now; you may be sitting alone in a corner of darkness. You may be facing temptation and problems that are too great to bear. You may find yourself out on a stormy sea and you feel like your little bark is going down.

I have some good news for you, Christian friends. "He saw them toiling in rowing." He sees you. He knows your problems. You don't have to send up a flare to let Him know. He already knows. Oh, that today you might commit your way to Him in a very definite way. That is something that so many of us need to do in times of darkness — just commit our way unto Him. "He saw them toiling in rowing." Only Mark, by the way, records that. Then we find that He came to them and He entered into the ship with them. And Mark says that they were "amazed in themselves beyond measure."

In the conclusion of this chapter we find that He went over to the land of Gennesaret.

> **And when they had passed over, they came into the land of Gennesaret, and drew to the shore.**
>
> **And when they were come out of the ship, straightway they knew him,**

Now I want you to listen to this very carefully in conclusion:

> **And ran through that whole region round about, and**

began to carry about in beds those that were sick, where they heard he was.

And whithersoever he entered, into villages, or cities, or country, they laid the sick in the streets, and besought him that they might touch if it were but the border of his garment: and as many as touched him were made whole [Mark 6:53-56].

You and I today can't even envisage the number of sick people that He had healed. I understand there is one denomination that has offered one thousand dollars to anybody who will come forward and show that he has been healed by a "faith healer." I understand the thousand dollars has never been taken. It's amazing, isn't it, when you hear all this propaganda today that is going around. In Jesus' day one could have brought together thousands of people that He had healed. My friend, He was genuine. It was real. That is the reason the enemy never denied that He performed miracles.

CHAPTER 7

This chapter carries out the theme of Mark which is to show that the Lord Jesus is God's Servant who is doing God's will. He is a Man of action and He is doing the things that would appeal to the Roman of that day and to any person who is interested in getting a job done. That is the wonderful thing about Him as a Saviour; He can save, and He is the only One who can.

The Inter-Testament period is that time between the close of the Old Testament and the opening of the New Testament in which many changes took place. It was one of the most eventful periods in the history of the nation Israel. During the time of their captivity and in this period between the Testaments after they had returned to the land, there was a development of new groups and parties not mentioned in the Old Testament. There were the Pharisees, the Sadducees, the scribes, and the Herodians.

Scribes — The scribes had a good beginning. Evidently Ezra was a scribe and the founder of that group. They were the professional expounders of the Law. However, by the time of our Lord they had become "hair-splitters" and were more concerned with the *letter* of the Law than with the *spirit* of the Law.

That, I think, is one of the great problems we have today. There has been put into the interpretation of the laws in this country this "hair-splitting" method and the philosophical interpretation that was never intended in the law. I believe that is what has come out of certain law schools in the East. As a result, our legal system and our political system are in the mess we find today. That is what had happened to religion in our Lord's day.

Pharisees — The Pharisees also had a good beginning. They arose to defend the Jewish way of life against all foreign influences. They were strict legalists, they believed in the Old Testament, and they were nationalists in politics. They wanted to bring in the coming of the Kingdom of Heaven (or the Kingdom of God) upon the earth.

Sadducees — The Sadducees were made up of the wealthy and socially-minded. They had no spiritual depth. They wanted to get rid of tradition. They rejected the supernatural and were opposed to the Pharisees who accepted the supernatural and accepted the Old Testament. They were closely akin to the Greek Epicureans.

Herodians — The Herodians were a party in the days of Jesus who arose as political opportunists. They were strictly a party to try to keep the Herods on the throne.

This background will help us understand the incident before us.

Then came together unto him the Parisees, and certain of the scribes, which came from Jerusalem [Mark 7:1].

You will notice that our Lord has made such an impression that these men are drawn out of Jerusalem, and they have come to the place where He is ministering in Galilee. Also they will come across the Jordan River into the area of the Decapolis; that is, the area of ten cities. We'll see that in a moment.

And when they saw some of his disciples eat bread with defiled, that is to say, with unwashen, hands, they found fault.

For the Pharisees, and all the Jews, except they wash their hands oft, eat not, holding the tradition of the elders.

And when they come from the market, except they wash, they eat not. And many other things there be, which they have received to hold, as the washing of cups, and pots, brasen vessels, and of tables [Mark 7:2-4].

Let us stop to look at this for just a moment because it is quite interesting. There is a crisis arising about the Person of Jesus. Back in Mark 6:30 we read that the apostles had gathered themselves around Jesus and had told Him all the things that they had done after He had sent them out. They had come back and reported to Him. Now also the scribes and the Pharisees are coming out and gathering about Him. There is bound to be a confrontation here between the Lord Jesus and His followers and the Pharisees and their followers. One group is made up of His friends, His followers, who love Him. The second group is comprised of His enemies who seek to destroy Him.

It has always been this way. There are two groups: those who trust Him and those who reject Him. To be personal, which group are you in? That makes all the difference in the world. The question is not whether you are a member of a church or have been through some ceremony; rather it is what is your relationship to Jesus Christ? That is the all-important question.

Now this obviously was a special delegation from Jerusalem. They had been sent to Galilee to spy on Jesus. They were the intellectual opponents sent to trap the Lord Jesus. The way that our Lord defended Himself is to me another proof of His deity — "Never man spake like this man" was the testimony of His enemies (John 7:46). Of course, it wasn't difficult for them to find some fault because the Lord Jesus entirely ignored their traditions.

Now what was their tradition? They were not simply criticizing the disciples because of a breach of etiquette, but for the fact that the Lord was not having them keep the traditions, which were their interpretation of the Old Testament. This referred to a ceremonial cleansing and hadn't anything to do with sanitary measures. Mark explains for the benefit of the Romans that this custom of ceremonial cleansing was peculiar to Israel; and it was.

God had given to Israel a great deal of information about cleansing. In the Old Testament, in the book of Leviticus, there is a great deal of instruction about cleansing. It was very important because God was teaching them the great lesson that a sinner had to be cleansed before he could enjoy fellowship with a holy God. But the Pharisees had built a great tradition that was supposed to be an interpretation of the Mosaic Law, and some of them even contended that Moses had given them the traditions when he gave them the Law. In time, these traditions became the interpretation of the Law, and eventually there was a wide departure in the traditions from what had been the intent of the Law.

In our passage here, some of this tradition is given in detail. They would ceremonially wash the cups and pots and brasen vessels and the tables. All of this was a burdensome sort of thing and was an entirely outward performance. The word used for "washing" is *baptism*. They baptized cups, pots, religious objects, even tables. Now this is religion with a vengeance, friends, and you can see that one could get so involved in going through a ritual of religion that one would forget the whole purpose — which is that a person must be made *right* with God before a relationship can be established. We find the same kind of thing today. So many people will argue points of religion when it is the Person of Jesus Christ that should be our concern. Now let's go on:

Then the Pharisees and scribes asked him, Why walk not thy disciples according to the tradition of the elders, but eat bread with unwashen hands? [Mark 7:5].

This accusation which they lodge against His disciples was, of course, really an accusation against Him personally, because these were His followers. Now notice how our Lord deals with them — and it isn't tenderly at all!

He answered and said unto them, Well hath Esaias prophesied of you hypocrites, as it is written, This people honoureth me with their lips, but their heart is far from me [Mark 7:6].

I wouldn't say that is gentle. A hypocrite is one who is just acting a part; it is a word used for actors on the stage. They were going through a religious ritual without experiencing any reality at all. The lips and the heart might as well have belonged to two separate persons. They had no more heart experience than a wooden dummy upon the knee of a ventriloquist.

My friend, there are a lot of people who are just going through a ritual in church today. The heart must be involved if it is genuine. "That if thou shalt confess with thy mouth the Lord Jesus, and shalt believe in thine heart that God hath raised him from the dead, thou shalt be saved. For with the heart man believeth unto righteousness; and with the mouth confession is made unto salvation" (Rom. 10:9, 10). Oh, people get involved today in creeds and church confessions and public worship, dress and even 'separation.' All of this can become a matter of tradi-

tion and not a direct and personal dealing with the Lord Jesus
Christ.

> **Howbeit in vain do they worship me, teaching for doctrines the commandments of men [Mark 7:7].**

Worship is empty when the rules of men are substituted for the
Word of God. So now we come to the very heart of the matter.

> **For laying aside the commandment of God, ye hold the tradition of men, as the washing of pots and cups: and many other such like things ye do.**

> **And he said unto them, Full well ye reject the commandment of God, that ye may keep your own tradition [Mark 7:8,9].**

Here was the whole issue. They were substituting traditions of
men for the Word of God. A tradition may actually be good and
may be established for a very good reason. However, it becomes
evil when it is a substitute for the Word of God in later
generations. And that is what has happened to these people here.

I think this is the reason that so many denominations today
have departed from the Word of God. They first substituted a
creed for the Word of God. Then they began to substitute the
word of men and the thinking of men and their own little ritual
and their own little denomination. Before long, the Word of God
went out the window. This has happened again and again.

> **For Moses said, Honour thy father and thy mother; and, Whoso curseth father or mother, let him die the death:**

> **But ye say, If a man shall say to his father or mother, It is Corban, that is to say, a gift, by whatsoever thou mightest be profited by me; he shall be free [Mark 7:10,11].**

Now He is giving them an example of what they were doing.
Moses had said in the Law that they were to honor their father
and their mother. But their tradition permitted them to escape
the responsibility to their parents. If a man did not want to help
his father and mother when they became old and needy, he
would dedicate his possessions to the priest in the temple and it

was called "Corban" which means, a gift. At the man's death, his estate went to the temple and he was relieved of his responsibility to his parents.

> **And ye suffer him no more to do ought for his father or his mother;**
>
> **Making the word of God of none effect through your tradition, which ye have delivered: and many such like things do ye [Mark 7:12,13].**

He's saying that this tradition was pernicious and it directly contradicted the intent of the Law of God which was to honor their father and mother.

There is a great danger today that people will give to any group or organization that has appealed to them. There are literally thousands of Christian organizations that have men out in the field, combing the highways and byways to find people to give to an organization. There is a grave danger in that. There are certain personal responsibilities that people must fulfill.

As we go on down the passage before us we see He goes into detail.

> **And when he had called all the people unto him, he said unto them, Hearken unto me every one of you, and understand:**
>
> **There is nothing from without a man, that entering into him can defile him: but the things which come out of him, those are they that defile the man [Mark 7:14, 15].**

He is differentiating that which is external and that which is internal and is pointing out what is real. He shows here that religion is not something that you can rub on as you do a salve. It is not something that you eat or refrain from eating.

You'll notice then that He went into the house and his disciples came to Him and asked Him about the parable.

> **And he saith unto them, Are ye so without understanding also? Do ye not perceive, that whatsoever thing from without entereth into the man, it cannot defile him;**

Because it entereth not into his heart, but into the belly, and goeth out into the draught, purging all meats?

And he said, That which cometh out of the man, that defileth the man [Mark 7:18-20].

Let's really take a look at what does come out of man:

For from within, out of the heart of man, proceed evil thoughts, adulteries, fornications, murders,

Thefts, covetousness, wickedness, deceit, lasciviousness, an evil eye, blasphemy, pride, foolishness:

All these evil things come from within, and defile the man [Mark 7:21-23].

I'll guarantee you that if you will buy the morning paper wherever you live and will read it through, you will find that this is what came out of man during the last twenty-four hours:

Evil thoughts

Adulteries and fornications — unlawful sex relations

Murders (anger is also murder)

Thefts (loafing on the job is also stealing)

Covetousness — grasping and greediness for material things and positions

Wickedness — all the acts that are intended to hurt people

Deceit — the pretense that people put up

Lasciviousness — sensuality

Evil eye — envy

Blasphemy — slander against God or man

Pride (God hates this above all else)

Foolishness — acts done without any respect of God or man

These all come out of the heart of man and that is why the Lord Jesus says, "Ye must be born again."

And from thence he arose, and went into the borders of Tyre and Sidon, and entered into an house, and would have no man know it: but he could not be hid.

For a certain woman, whose young daughter had an unclean spirit, heard of him, and came and fell at his feet:

The woman was a Greek, a Syrophenician by nation; and she besought him that he would cast forth the devil out of her daughter.

But Jesus said unto her, Let the children first be filled; for it is not meet to take the children's bread, and to cast it unto the dogs.

And she answered and said unto him, Yes, Lord: yet the dogs under the table eat of the children's crumbs.

And he said unto her, For this saying go thy way; the devil is gone out of thy daughter.

And when she was come to her house, she found the devil gone out, and her daughter laid upon the bed [Mark 7:24-30].

We have had this incident before. You will recall that our Lord stepped out of His own land and met this woman who was a Greek and a citizen of Tyre. She came to Jesus in faith. And the word "daughter" here is the diminutive form which means she was just a little girl. At first, our Lord's treatment of her may appear brutal, but you will remember that when we studied this in the Gospel of Matthew, we showed the dispensational interpretation which is actually the revelation of a tremendous truth. And I think here something else tremendous is also revealed and that is the accuracy of the four Gospels. This woman is an outstanding example of faith in one who lives outside His land. And our Lord answered her petition. One wonders whether He came to that area for the specific purpose of answering the faith of this woman.

And again, departing from the coasts of Tyre and Sidon, he came unto the sea of Galilee, through the midst of the coasts of Decapolis [Mark 7:31].

Jesus leaves Tyre and Sidon, and goes through Decapolis on His way to the Sea of Galilee. *Decapolis* translated is Ten cities, a district containing ten cities, mostly on the East of the Jordan, in the area near the Sea of Galilee. The list includes the following:

Scythopolis	Gerasa	Dion
Hippos	Gadara	Canatha
Pella	Raphana	Philadelphia
Damascus		

I was at the ruins of Gerasa or Jerish, as it is called today. I thought, "My, this is one of the places where my Lord came and He taught." He had a tremendous ministry in this area. The crowds came into those cities.

And they bring unto him one that was deaf, and had an impediment in his speech; and they beseech him to put his hand upon him.

And he took him aside from the multitude, and put his fingers into his ears, and he spit, and touched his tongue;

And looking up to heaven, he sighed, and saith unto him, Ephphatha, that is, Be opened.

And straightway his ears were opened, and the string of his tongue was loosed, and he spake plain.

And he charged them that they should tell no man: but the more he charged them, so much the more a great deal they published it;

And were beyond measure astonished, saying, He hath done all things well: he maketh both the deaf to hear, and the dumb to speak [Mark 7:32-37].

May I say, that all the things He did were done as aids to faith. The whole thought here reveals the fact that the condition of this man caused Jesus to use this method. His ears were first opened so that he could hear. After this it apparently was useless to try to get the crowd to remain silent. It was this miracle which brought about a great impetus in enlarging the ministry of Jesus, which had already broken all bounds.

At this time pressure upon Jesus was humanly unbearable. In spite of the pressure put upon Jesus, the burdens of the multitudes, the tensions of the times, the long busy days, and the weariness of the body, the crowd could say, "He hath done all things well." We just add our word of agreement to this and say a hearty amen.

Friends, He still does all things well today!

CHAPTER 8

The eighth chapter is about the same length as the seventh chapter. It still carries out the great theme of Mark with the emphasis upon action. Jesus feeds the 4,000 in the coasts of Decapolis, the Pharisees ask for a sign at Dalmanutha, the friends of a blind man ask Jesus to touch his eyes at Bethsaida, Peter makes his confession of faith in Caesarea Philippi. What the Lord Jesus did was important to the Romans, and it is important to us today. Is the Lord Jesus able to save to the uttermost? Can He do the job? He is the Servant of Jehovah, and we find that He can do the job.

We find in this chapter that our Lord does a lot of moving around, and there weren't good highways in that day. That land is a small land, but when you reduce the speed down to walking speed, it's a pretty sizeable land. And He travelled by walking.

Some people feel that the feeding of the four thousand which opens this chapter is a duplication of the feeding of the five thousand, and they practically ignore it. This has caused some to say that the feeding of the four thousand is the neglected miracle of Jesus.

When the critic comes to this parable, in his usual way he seeks to rid the Bible of the supernatural. His explanation of this miracle is that it was included after the feeding of the five thousand to strengthen the claim of the apostles that Jesus was a miracle worker. Obviously, if this were true, the second miracle would be greater than the first — instead of four thousand, it would be nearer ten thousand. When men fabricate they exaggerate. And here it is restraint, by the way.

The two miracles of feeding the multitudes are strikingly similar in several features. He feeds the thousands, one time it is five and the next time it is four. But there are seven points of dissimilarity that we need to call to your attention.

1. In the first instance the multitude had been with the Lord one day; in the second instance it had been three days.

2. Upon the first occasion the disciples were told to "go and see" what supplies were available, while upon the other they were ready with the information before they were asked.

3. When the five thousand were fed there were five loaves and two fishes, while for the four thousand there were seven loaves and a few fishes.

4. The first time, which was near the Passover, the multitude was told to sit in companies "upon the green grass," while the second time, later in the year when the green of the Near East would be burnt by the oriental sun, they were instructed to sit "on the ground" (literally, "on the earth").

5. In the first instance our Lord is said to have "blessed . . . the loaves," while upon the second occasion He is said to have given thanks, first for the loaves, and later to have "blessed" the fish.

6. After the five thousand were fed twelve baskets of fragments remained, but when the four thousand were satisfied there were seven baskets over.

7. Obviously, the number that was fed was different in each instance.

It seems that the sharp contrast between the two is found in the time that Jesus fed the multitudes. In the feeding of the five thousand, it was at the conclusion of the first day. Jesus had been teaching them, but according to John, He followed the feeding of the five thousand with the discourse of the Bread of Life. This important discourse was sort of an after-dinner speech, you see. In the feeding of the four thousand, the multitude had been with Jesus for three days listening to His teaching. The physical food followed the teaching. In other words, the crowd had not come out to eat but to hear the teaching of Jesus.

I think this is an important lesson for us. Are we using church dinners to get the crowd? If so, then our motive is wrong. Many churches can get people out in the middle of the week only if they have a banquet. Some Bible classes depend upon the food to draw people in for the message. Can God bless such efforts regardless of how pure the motive? Well, I'll let you answer it. The end does not always justify the means.

As we begin to read now, notice that "in those days" places this incident during the time He was in the Decapolis. The multitude evidently had followed Jesus into a desert place which was convenient for teaching but not readily accessible to supplies. *Great* multitudes are following Him now.

> In those days the multitude being very great, and having nothing to eat, Jesus called his disciples unto him, and saith unto them,
>
> I have compassion on the multitude, because they have now been with me three days, and have nothing to eat:
>
> And if I send them away fasting to their own houses, they will faint by the way: for divers of them came from far.
>
> And his disciples answered him, From whence can a man satisfy these men with bread here in the wilderness?
>
> And he asked them, How many loaves have ye? And they said, Seven.
>
> And he commanded the people to sit down on the ground: and he took the seven loaves, and gave thanks, and brake, and gave to his disciples to set before them; and they did set them before the people [Mark 8:1-6].

There is something quite interesting here. It looks as though the disciples had forgotten about His feeding of the five thousand. I'm of the opinion that many of us have the same kind of experience. God does some very gracious and good thing for us and we forget it by the next time. When a new emergency arises, we find ourselves neophytes; that is, it is all brand new to us again. That has been my experience as I have periodic X-rays made of my lungs to see whether the cancer has spread. And every time it is a new experience for me and I must confess that every time I am frightened. So I have really a fellow-feeling for these disciples.

They had made an inventory of the crowd, though, because they knew how many loaves there were. Maybe they were expecting Jesus to repeat the miracle of the five thousand. This time there were more loaves for fewer people but it was still true,

"What are these among so many?" And who had the loaves this
time? We don't know. Some unknown person had them and even
though we don't know who he was, he will have his reward someday.

In this instance they sat on the bare ground, while at the
feeding of the five thousand they had been told to sit on the grass,
as I had mentioned. And how many fish? It just says "a few small
fishes." The number really is unimportant, and He's not count-
ing the fish. When God is in it, you will notice, there is always a
surplus. Whether He feeds five or four thousand, He doesn't give
them just a snack but He gives them a full dinner. Incidentally,
if we add one woman and one child for each of the men, we
probably would be nearer to the actual number of people who
were fed — about twelve thousand.

> **And straightway he entered into a ship with his dis-
> ciples, and came into the parts of Dalmanutha [Mark
> 8:10].**

The location of Dalmanutha cannot be ascertained accurately.
Apparently it was on the coast of the Sea of Galilee and they had
to cross the sea to get to it, which means they came to the west
side. They travelled by boat and evidently the spot was
somewhere on the northwest coast. Now the bloodhounds of hate
are on His trail again.

> **And the Pharisees came forth, and began to question
> with him, seeking of him a sign from heaven, tempting
> him.**
>
> **And he sighed deeply in his spirit, and saith, Why doth
> this generation seek after a sign? verily I say unto you,
> There shall no sign be given unto this generation.**
>
> **And he left them, and entering into the ship again
> departed to the other side.**
>
> **Now the disciples had forgotten to take bread, neither
> had they in the ship with them more than one loaf.**
>
> **And he charged them, saying, Take heed, beware of the
> leaven of the Pharisees, and of the leaven of Herod
> [Mark 8:11-15].**

In the Scriptures leaven represents wrong or evil teaching; it never means the Gospel. One of the fallacious things that is being taught today is that leaven represents the Gospel in the parable of the woman who hid leaven in three measures of meal (Matthew 13:33). The Gospel symbolizes the meal, and the leaven which represents wrong teaching was hidden in it. It is the process of making something taste good to the natural man. Actually, what is liberalism? It all came into existence by the pulpit trying to please the unsaved church members. And today we have a lot of men trying to please the congregation, even when they are unsaved. And that, may I say, is putting leaven in — that is, mixing wrong teaching with the truth of the Gospel. The only kind of bread they will eat is that which has leaven because leaven makes bread taste good. I was brought up on hot biscuits, friends, and the natural man likes them. Leaven is the evil that is put in. And here He is warning them about the wrong teaching of the Pharisees and Herod.

Having eyes, see ye not? and having ears, hear ye not? and do ye not remember? [Mark 8:18].

I've been a preacher for a long time, friends, and sometimes I discover something that startles me. There will be some person whom I think knows spiritual truth, yet they have missed the entire thought. They don't get it at all and one wonders where they have been. There are people who have been studying the Bible for years and who are like that. They are like these apostles who have ears, yet hear not.

When I brake the five loaves among five thousand, how many baskets full of fragments took ye up? They say unto him, Twelve.

And when the seven among four thousand, how many baskets full of fragments took ye up? And they said, Seven.

And he said unto them, How is it that ye do not understand? [Mark 8:19-21].

The Word of God is the bread of life because the Word of God reveals Him. We are to feed on the Bible and to beware of false teaching. I think that ought to be clear to us here in the teaching that He gives.

And he cometh to Bethsaida; and they bring a blind man unto him, and besought him to touch him [Mark 8:22].

Here is another one of these remarkable miracles of our Lord. He assented to their request by touching his eyes. But you notice that He led the blind man out of town. Had Bethsaida, where many of His mighty works had been performed, become like Nazareth where He could no longer perform might works? Surely there is no medicinal value in saliva, but the Lord uses this to increase the faith of this man. Let us read this and learn the spiritual truth for us here.

And he took the blind man by the hand, and led him out of the town; and when he had spit on his eyes, and put his hands upon him, he asked him if he saw ought.

And he looked up, and said, I see men as trees, walking.

After that he put his hands again upon his eyes, and made him look up: and he was restored, and saw every man clearly.

And he sent him away to his house, saying, Neither go into the town, nor tell it to any in the town [Mark 8:23-26].

This place of Bethsaida had already had judgment pronounced upon it (Matthew 11:21). Now there's something in this miracle we want to look at very carefully. Why did He use this method? Couldn't He have opened the eyes of this man as He did in other instances? Of course, He could have. He could have made this man see clearly at the very beginning. But there is a lesson for the man and a lesson here for us.

There are three stages in this case:

1. Blindness. We are all first spiritually blind. Like the blind man we can say, "Once I was blind, but now I can see." But you'll notice that He gained only partial sight, and only Mark tells us this.

2. Partial sight. Is this not our condition today? "Now we see through a glass darkly, but then face to face" (I Corinthians 13:12). Every now and then I get a letter from some person who

gives me to understand that they have great spiritual discernment. They are way up there with the upper ten, and sometimes they say they think that's where I am. But I have a confession to make to you. I only see through a glass darkly. There are many things I don't understand.

There are some people who don't feel that way. They think they know all of the things that there are to know. That is one of the curses of some of our good Bible-teaching churches. I was a pastor for a great many years. I had members who never bothered to come to mid-week Bible study. Do you know why? They already knew more than I know. Now that may be true, but the tragic thing was that they thought they knew more than they actually knew.

Socrates, in his day, made the statement that he was the wisest of the Athenians. That shocked everybody because he was a very humble man. So they asked him what he meant. And he said something like this, "Well there are a great many of the Athenians who think they know, and I know I do not know. And since I know that I do not know, I am the wisest of the Athenians."

May I say to you that there are a lot of the saints today who think they know. But Paul says that we see through a glass darkly, and that is our state in this life. But eventually when we come into His presence we shall know as we are known. I'll surely be glad when I get over there where I'm going to know something!

3. Perfect sight. The third stage is perfect vision. We'll get our 20-20 spiritual vision when we come into His presence, and that's when we'll really be able to see. You'll notice that when our Lord had finished, He had healed this man perfectly.

There is something here that I don't have time to develop fully today, but have you ever noticed the different methods that our Lord used in opening the eyes of the blind? Here at Bethsaida when He healed the blind man, he touched his eyes. So this man had an experience. I imagine that he would have organized the "Metho-rene" church and they would sing "The Touch of His Hand on Mine." When Jesus healed blind Bartimaeus He didn't touch him at all but just told him from a distance, and faith alone opened his eyes. I suppose he would have organized the

"Congreterian" church and they would sing, of course, "Only Believe." But the man who had been born blind was told to go and wash in the pool of Siloam and that's an entirely different method according to John, chapter 9. So this man would have organized a "Siloam-Baptian" church and they would sing, "Shall We Gather at the River." You say that that is absurd. Sure is. Absurd for that day, but today that is exactly what is being done. May I say to you that here is a lesson for us.

And Jesus went out, and his disciples, into the towns of Caesarea Philippi: and by the way he asked his disciples, saying unto them, Whom do men say that I am? [Mark 8:27].

The important thing here is, who is Jesus? Jesus wanted to know men's estimate of Him.

WHAT THINK YE OF CHRIST?

"What think ye of Christ?" is the test
To try both your state and your scheme;
You cannot be right in the rest,
Unless you think rightly of Him.

Friends, to be united to Him, joined to Him, is the important thing. We are to enjoy a right relationship with Jesus Christ.

If you look on a map, you will find three Caesareas. Caesarea Philippi is located to the north of the Sea of Galilee. The Lord Jesus is in the north and He is in a position from which He is going to turn and begin a movement directly toward Jerusalem and the cross.

And they answered, John the Baptist: but some say, Elias; and others, One of the prophets [Mark 8:28].

There was much confusion regarding His person. All opinions were high, but fell short of who He is.

And he saith unto them, But whom say ye that I am? And Peter answereth and saith unto him, Thou art the Christ [Mark 8:29].

This was their final examination for the first phase of His ministry. They were within six months now of the cross.

This is the finest thing that Simon Peter ever said. He spoke for the group. Mark gives us only a fragment of the confession. "Christ" is not a name. *Jesus* is His name. *Christ* is a title. In the Hebrew, it was the *Messiah*, which means the Anointed One. This title gathers up all the rich meaning of the Old Testament. It is a fragment with fullness. Compare Micah 5:2, Isaiah 7:14, Psalm 2:2, Psalm 45:6,7, and Malachi 3:1. These are but a few of the many Old Testament references. Jesus came to reveal God.

And he charged them that they should tell no man of him [Mark 8:30].

Why this strange admonition? They were to wait until the Gospel story was complete. Notice the next verse.

And he began to teach them, that the Son of man must suffer many things, and be rejected of the elders, and of the chief priests, and scribes, and be killed, and after three days rise again [Mark 8:31].

Jesus did not reveal His Person apart from His work of redemption. Salvation depends on who He is and what He did.

The final phase of their training begins here. It was at Caesarea Philippi that He first revealed His cross to them.

And he spake that saying openly. And Peter took him, and began to rebuke him [Mark 8:32].

Even now they were unprepared to receive it. This is the worst thing Simon Peter ever said.

But when he had turned about and looked on his disciples, he rebuked Peter, saying, Get thee behind me, Satan: for thou savourest not the things that be of God, but the things that be of men [Mark 8:33].

Jesus attributed this statement to Satan. Satan denies the value of the death of Jesus.

And when he had called the people unto him with his disciples also, he said unto them, Whosoever will come after me, let him deny himself, and take up his cross, and follow me.

For whosoever will save his life shall lose it; but whosoever shall lose his life for my sake and the gospel's, the same shall save it.

For what shall it profit a man, if he shall gain the whole world, and lose his own soul?

Or what shall a man give in exchange for his soul?

Whosoever therefore shall be ashamed of me and of my words in this adulterous and sinful generation; of him also shall the Son of man be ashamed, when he cometh in the glory of his Father with the holy angels [Mark 8:34-38].

The Lord does not reveal His Person apart from His work of redemption. After Peter confessed who He is and they truly recognized Him, He immediately told them, "The Son of man must suffer many things, and be rejected of the elders, and of the chief priests, and scribes, and be killed, and after three days rise again" (Mark 8:31). And then He gives the passage we have quoted. Here He is not putting down a condition of salvation, but stating the position of those who are saved. This is what He is talking about. "Whosoever therefore shall be ashamed of Me . . ." What kind of Christian are *you* today? Are you one who ackowledges Him and serves Him and attempts to glorify Him? My friend, this is all important in these days in which we live.

CHAPTER 9

We come today to the ninth chapter of the Gospel of Mark, and we have again the account of the transfiguration. This can be found in the first three Gospels, the synoptic Gospels. Then Mark tells us in detail that while the transfiguration was going on at the top of the mountain, there was complete failure of the disciples at the foot of the mountain. They could not cast the demon out of the boy. Then Jesus again announces His death and the disciples dispute as to who should be greatest. Jesus rebukes their party spirit and warns against hell. So this is another chapter just loaded with dynamite in the Gospel of action.

Mark is customarily briefer in his account than the other evangelists, but he gives the longest account of the transfiguration. It is interesting to ponder why he would emphasize it. It is our judgment that the transfiguration sets forth the perfect humanity of Christ and was not given to set forth His deity. As we said, the synoptic Gospels all relate it, but John does not. John's Gospel, which sets forth the deity of Christ, does not give the account of the transfiguration.

You will remember that in the last verse of chapter 16 in Matthew, Jesus said, "There be some standing here, which shall not taste of death, till they see the Son of man coming in his kingdom." There are all sorts of interpretations of that, but I think it is very clear that our Lord had definite reference to His transfiguration. Two men who were there, Peter and John, make reference to it. Peter says in II Peter 1:16-18: "For we have not followed cunningly devised fables, when we made known unto you the power and coming of our Lord Jesus Christ, but were eyewitnesses of his majesty. For he received from God the Father honour and glory, when there came such a voice to him from the excellent glory, This is my beloved Son, in whom I am well pleased. And this voice which came from heaven we heard, when we were with him in the holy mount." He is saying that they were witnesses of the power and coming of our Lord Jesus Christ. When? At the transfiguration!

> And he said unto them, Verily I say unto you, That there
> be some of them that stand here, which shall not taste of
> death, till they have seen the kingdom of God come with
> power [Mark 9:1].

I believe that the reason this is stated at this particular juncture before His death and resurrection was for us to understand
that whether He went to the cross or not, the Kingdom is in His
hands. He could have stepped off this earth back to heaven and
He would have been the sovereign Ruler of the universe. But that
way He couldn't have saved you and He couldn't have saved me.
I'm not going to develop that further, but that is important.

> And after six days Jesus taketh with him Peter, and
> James, and John, and leadeth them up into an high
> mountain apart by themselves: and he was transfigured
> before them [Mark 9:2].

Of course, the question arises as to why He took these three
men. Let me say first that He didn't take them because they
were His little pets, or that they were superior to the others. I
think that they were the weakest of the apostles, and He had to
carry them along with Him like babies or they would not have
come along at all.

I was noticing a mother go down the street who had three
children with her. She was carrying one, she was leading one by
the hand, and one was walking behind her. She'd have to stop
every now and then for him to catch up. I watched them as they
made very slow progress down the street. I thought to myself,
That little fellow following her surely is taking a lot of time. But
then I realized that the one she was carrying couldn't go along at
all unless she carried him. I feel that Peter, James, and John are
rather like that. They seemed to be an exclusive group, but I
think they were just babies, and He had to carry them. So He
took them in for the transfiguration.

Peter says that they were eyewitnesses of His majesty. This is
it. This is the glorified Christ as He will come some day to this
earth. This also, friends, is a picture of what you and I will be
someday. We are told that we shall be like Him (I John 3:2). You
will recall that John says, "We beheld his glory, the glory as of
the only begotten of the Father" (John 1:14).

The word "transfigured" here is the Greek word *metamorphoom*, or metamorphose in English. The transfiguration took place in the body of Jesus — it wasn't just a light or some effect produced from the outside. The transfiguration was the light that shone from within. I rather think that Adam and Eve were clothed like that, with a light from within. The transfiguration teaches, therefore, the perfect humanity of Jesus and not His deity.

And his raiment became shining, exceeding white as snow; so as no fuller on earth can white them [Mark 9:3].

His raiment became white. It was whiter than was even believable, because the light came from within, you see. The word "fuller" means a cloth dresser, and refers to the laundry. In other words, no modern washday miracle could have produced such brightness. All of it came from within.

And there appeared unto them Elias with Moses: and they were talking with Jesus [Mark 9:4].

Elias is the Greek form of *Elijah*. Elijah was the representative of the prophets. Moses was the representative of the Law. We are told that both the Law and the prophets bore testimony of the death of Jesus. Luke tells us that they talked about the decease of Jesus. We know that Moses knew of Christ because we are told in Hebrews 11:26 concerning Moses: "Esteeming the reproach of Christ greater riches than the treasures in Egypt: for he had respect unto the recompence of the reward." Moses knew He was coming. All of the prophets spoke of His suffering and the glory that should follow.

And Peter answered and said to Jesus, Master, it is good for us to be here: and let us make three tabernacles; one for thee, and one for Moses, and one for Elias.

For he wist not what to say; for they were sore afraid [Mark 9:5,6].

Peter was the spokesman for them here just as he always was the spokesman. And Simon Peter generally spoke when he didn't know what to say. I think that Simon Peter put his foot in his mouth time and time again and he certainly did it here.

And there was a cloud that overshadowed them: and a voice came out of the cloud, saying, This is my beloved Son: hear him [Mark 9:7].

All attention now is focused on the Lord Jesus Christ. His Word is final. We don't put Moses or Elijah on a par with Him.

And suddenly, when they had looked round about, they saw no man any more, save Jesus only with themselves [Mark 9:8].

By the way, that "Jesus Only" is a marvelous headline, is it not? "Jesus Only" is not only a headline in Mark's Gospel, but it ought to be a headline in the lives of believers today. In a brief way he states such great and weighty words — Jesus Only!

And as they came down from the mountain, he charged them that they should tell no man what things they had seen, till the Son of man were risen from the dead [Mark 9:9].

You see, the death and resurrection of Christ must go along with this story. The transfiguration saves no man. It presents the ideal or the goal. But that goal can only come through the death of Christ upon the cross and through His resurrection from the dead. And you will notice that He always puts His death and resurrection together.

And they kept that saying with themselves, questioning one with another what the rising from the dead should mean [Mark 9:10].

They were entirely ignorant of the resurrection. At the time of Jesus' resurrection they rushed to the cemetery but they did not expect to see a living Saviour. You don't go to the graveyard to see the living, but to pay respect to the dead.

And they asked him, saying, Why say the scribes that Elias must first come?

And he answered and told them, Elias verily cometh first, and restoreth all things; and how it is written of the Son

of man, that he must suffer many things, and be set at nought.

But I say unto you, That Elias is indeed come, and they have done unto him whatsoever they listed, as it is written of him [Mark 9:11-13].

Our Lord made it clear that when anyone would say, "Well, after all, Jesus could not establish the Kingdom because the prophet said that Elijah must come first," that John the Baptist had come in the spirit of Elijah. If they had accepted Jesus as the Messiah, John would have been the fulfillment of the prophecy. However, since they did not accept Jesus as their Messiah at His first coming, the prophecy of Elijah as His forerunner would be fulfilled at His second coming.

Now, from this glorious scene on the mountain top, we go down to total defeat of the disciples at the foot of the mountain.

And when he came to his disciples, he saw a great multitude about them, and the scribes questioning with them.

And straightway all the people, when they beheld him, were greatly amazed, and running to him saluted him.

And he asked the scribes, What question ye with them?

And one of the multitude answered and said, Master, I have brought unto thee my son, which hath a dumb spirit;

And wheresoever he taketh him, he teareth him: and he foameth, and gnasheth with his teeth, and pineth away: and I spake to thy disciples that they should cast him out; and they could not [Mark 9:14-18].

This is actually a picture of Christendom today. The Lord Jesus has already gone into the presence of the Father and is there in His glorified body. His apostles are there with Him. They have already gone on, and most of the church has already gone on. Moses and Elijah are there today. The mount of transfiguration pictures heaven today.

But look at this poor earth and see the problem down here.

This boy represents a mad earth today. I tell you, I believe that if we could get off and look at this earth and behold it as God looks at it, and probably as the angels look at it, we would come to the conclusion that man on this earth must be mad. He appears to be demon possessed by the way he is acting and the things he is doing down here. The sad thing is that the man brought the boy to the disciples, but they couldn't do anything. And the tragic thing about this hour is that the church is helpless in the presence of the world's need.

Right now, the organized church in desperation is reaching out, protesting and marching and getting involved in all kinds of things, and the world is actually criticizing the church because they feel it should get even more involved. But social matters are not our business! We ought to be able to help a poor demon-possessed boy today by presenting a Saviour to him who will make him rational and who will bring him into a right relationship with God. Unfortunately, the same thing has to be said of the church, "They could not." The disciples could not and we cannot. So the Lord Jesus says,

> O faithless generation, how long shall I be with you? how long shall I suffer you? bring him unto me [Mark 9:19].

What a wonderful statement! Bring him unto Me! We are attempting to do everything except bring lost men to Jesus Christ.

> And they brought him unto him: and when he saw him, straightway the spirit tare him; and he fell on the ground, and wallowed foaming.
>
> And he asked his father, How long is it ago since this came unto him? And he said, Of a child.
>
> And ofttimes it hath cast him into the fire, and into the waters, to destroy him: but if thou canst do any thing, have compassion on us, and help us [Mark 9:20-22].

This case, friends, is a bad case. It may not have been quite as bad as the case of the man among the tombs over in Gadara because he was a grown man and had been demon possessed for a long time. This was a boy, but had he gone on in this state he would probably have been as bad, if not worse, than the other case. So this father just casts himself upon the Lord Jesus on behalf of his tortured son. When we do that, friends, He'll do something to help.

Jesus said unto him, If thou canst believe, all things are possible to him that believeth [Mark 9:23].

The thought here is that Jesus turned to the father and asked him to believe — could the father have been responsible in any way for the condition of the boy? It is not a question of "if Thou canst do anything" — the Lord Jesus can do everything. The question is, "If thou canst believe." What about the father? The Lord Jesus told him that all things are possible to him that believeth.

And straightway the father of the child cried out, and said with tears, Lord, I believe; help thou mine unbelief [Mark 9:24].

Here is the father's desperate plea of faith!

When Jesus saw that the people came running together, he rebuked the foul spirit, saying unto him, Thou dumb and deaf spirit, I charge thee, come out of him, and enter no more into him.

And the spirit cried, and rent him sore, and came out of him: and he was as one dead; insomuch that many said, He is dead.

But Jesus took him by the hand, and lifted him up; and he arose [Mark 9:25-27].

The question arises here whether this also is a case of our Lord raising the dead. I am of the opinion it is, but I don't want to labor that point.

And when he was come into the house, his disciples asked him privately, Why could not we cast him out?

And he said unto them, This kind can come forth by nothing, but by prayer and fasting [Mark 9:28,29].

Now, in the Lord's answer to the disciples, we find that the word "fasting" is not in the better manuscripts. The emphasis is upon prayer. And today, friends, the church is weak because prayer is weak in the church.

And they departed thence, and passed through Galilee; and he would not that any man should know it.

For he taught his disciples, and said unto them, The Son of man is delivered into the hands of men, and they shall kill him; and after that he is killed, he shall rise the third day [Mark 9:30,31].

You will notice that He always puts His death and resurrection together.

But they understood not that saying, and were afraid to ask him [Mark 9:32].

They didn't quite understand this matter of being raised from the dead. Here He is talking about His own death for them and you would think that these men might have at least made some inquiry. They dared to dispute among themselves who would be greatest in the Kingdom after He had just announced His death. They should have been ashamed of their conduct here. This is not the first time He has announced His death and resurrection to them, and still they do not understand.

And he came to Capernaum: and being in the house he asked them, What was it that ye disputed among yourselves by the way?

But they held their peace: for by the way they had disputed among themselves, who should be the greatest.

And he sat down, and called the twelve, and saith unto them, If any man desire to be first, the same shall be last of all, and servant of all [Mark 9:33-35].

This is the profound spiritual principle of greatness.

And he took a child, and set him in the midst of them: and when he had taken him in his arms, he said unto them,

> **Whosoever shall receive one of such children in my name, receiveth me: and whosoever shall receive me, receiveth not me, but him that sent me [Mark 9:36, 37].**

He illustrates this principle with the child. Note that Jesus took the child in His arms.

> **And John answered him, saying, Master, we saw one casting out devils in thy name, and he followeth not us: and we forbad him, because he followeth not us.**

> **But Jesus said, Forbid him not: for there is no man which shall do a miracle in my name, that can lightly speak evil of me.**

> **For he that is not against us is on our part.**

> **For whosoever shall give you a cup of water to drink in my name, because ye belong to Christ, verily I say unto you, he shall not lose his reward [Mark 9:38-41].**

John is always thought of as a lady-like apostle but notice his fiery disposition here. Jesus rebukes any kind of sectarian spirit here. You will notice that the basis of unity which Jesus made is "in My name." That which is done in the name of Jesus cannot be denied by any follower. However, the label of "Jesus" is put on much today that actually is not "in His name."

Now notice that in verse 42, He comes back to the child that He has taken into His arms. This is tender, but it is severe upon those who offend a little child.

> **And whosoever shall offend one of these little ones that believe in me, it is better for him that a millstone were hanged about his neck, and he were cast into the sea [Mark 9:42].**

Then He adds this:

> **And if thy hand offend thee, cut it off: it is better for thee to enter into life maimed, than having two hands to go into hell, into the fire that never shall be quenched [Mark 9:43].**

Do you realize who it is here that is talking about hell? There are those today who say that He is the gentle Jesus. Friends, He is the only One who talked about hell. Paul never talked about it, but Jesus did. And since He did, it would be well for us to listen to Him. He said that there is a place, and it is called hell. I'm confident that it is a *place*, and it is a place just like He describes it.

Verses 44 and 46 are not in the better manuscripts. It might be well if we omit them.

Jesus talks about the hand, the foot, the eye.

> **And if thy foot offend thee, cut it off: it is better for thee to enter halt into life, than having two feet to be cast into hell, into the fire that never shall be quenched:**

> **And if thine eye offend thee, pluck it out: it is better for thee to enter into the kingdom of God with one eye, than having two eyes to be cast into hell fire [Mark 9:45,47].**

The eye can lead to sin. Think of Eve who first saw the tree was good for food.

> **For every one shall be salted with fire, and every sacrifice shall be salted with salt.**

> **Salt is good: but if the salt have lost his saltness, wherewith will ye season it? Have salt in yourselves, and have peace one with another [Mark 9:49,50].**

These are strange statements. The thought is that both fire and salt purify. Fire purifies by burning away the dross and impurities. Salt penetrates and burns out the corruption and stays the spread of impurities. If we have salt — the cleansing work of the Word of God — working within us, it sanctifies and brings peace.

CHAPTER 10

The first verse tells us that He arose from thence, and cometh into the coasts of Judaea by the farther side of Jordan. You will notice that there is a movement here in Mark. In fact, the geography in Mark is quite interesting. In Mark 9:30 we read that they departed thence, and passed through Galilee; and He would not that any man should know it. He was making His final departure from there and He certainly didn't want a big send-off. Now He comes into the coast of Judaea by the farther side of Jordan which means on the east side. That was in the area called Decapolis after the ten cities which were there. So we find Him by the farther side of Jordan. The people are coming to Him again, and He taught them "as He was wont." He's now making His final ascent to Jerusalem. The enemies, those bloodhounds of hate, are on His trail.

> **And he arose from thence, and cometh into the coasts of Judaea by the farther side of Jordan: and the people resort unto him again; and, as he was wont, he taught them again.**

> **And the Pharisees came to him, and asked him, Is it lawful for a man to put away his wife? tempting him [Mark 10:1,2].**

We need to understand that they do not ask this question because they want an answer. They are asking Him the question in order to trap Him. They had their own viewpoint concerning marriage and divorce; so they pose this trick question: "Is it lawful for a man to put away his wife?" It's a clever question and was really a live issue at this time because Herod had put away his wife and married his brother Philip's wife. John the Baptist had been beheaded because he had spoken out against it. So if Jesus answered no to their question, it would not only make Him contradict Moses, but it would bring Him into conflict with Herod. The death of Jesus was not to be determined on this issue. That's very important to see. On the other hand, if He said yes to their question, they could accuse Him of being lax in His teaching. So now notice His method. It always was His method and it was a good one. He countered with a question.

And he answered and said unto them, What did Moses command you?

And they said, Moses suffered to write a bill of divorcement, and to put her away [Mark 10:3,4].

He knew they would have to say that because back in Deuteronomy 24:1,2 there was the Mosaic Law: "When a man hath taken a wife, and married her, and it come to pass that she find no favour in his eyes, because he hath found some uncleanness in her: then let him write her a bill of divorcement, and give it in her hand, and send her out of his house. And when she is departed out of his house, she may go and be another man's wife."

Moses permitted divorce, as you can see. Now actually, it was not Moses' intention, nor was it God's intention for a man or a woman to get a divorce over some little, picayunish excuse. Actually, in time, the religious rulers interpreted it so that the wife burning the biscuits would be grounds for divorce.

Now our Lord goes back to that which is fundamental, and this is important to see. He turns it from a discussion of divorce to a discussion of marriage. And today that is the area into which we should move. I have so many questions from people asking about the grounds for divorce. When they are ready to get married, they never talk to the preacher. They are not interested in finding out whether he would approve or not; their only question is whether he will marry them. That is all they are concerned about.

The important thing to see here is that our Lord is going to discuss marriage with them. Notice how He handles it. He gives the reason God permitted divorce. It was because of sin that God granted divorce under the Mosaic Law.

And Jesus answered and said unto them, For the hardness of your heart he wrote you this precept.

But from the beginning of the creation God made them male and female.

For this cause shall a man leave his father and mother, and cleave to his wife;

And they twain shall be one flesh: so then they are no more twain, but one flesh.

What therefore God hath joined together, let not man put asunder [Mark 10:5-9].

What Jesus is saying here takes them back to God's ideal at the creation before sin entered the world. Divorce was not in His plan and program at that time. He had something better for man. It may likewise be said that murder was not in His plan, but murderers have been forgiven. Divorce is a sin, but divorced people can be forgiven. And I think that under certain circumstances divorced people can be remarried, friends; that is from a scriptural viewpoint. I don't know why we will forgive a murderer but often refuse to forgive a divorced person. We act almost as if they have committed the unpardonable sin. People who are saved after securing a divorce ought not to bear the stigma any more than any other sinner who has been saved. We are all sinners saved by grace. It just happens that divorce is their sin.

What He is saying in this section here is that marriage is a stronger tie than that of parent and child. A child may be disowned, and marriage may be broken by unfaithfulness. Jesus is showing here that marriage is something that God makes. God joins a couple together. This was the original intention of the Creator. Any violation of this is sin, but it is not the unpardonable sin, I can assure you.

The basic problem is marrying the wrong person. It looks to me like we are locking the stable after the horse is gone. There are people getting married who ought not to get married. This is the problem. The sin was that they got married in the first place. My Christian friend, marriage is something that God wants to arrange for you, if you will let Him.

And in the house his disciples asked him again of the same matter.

And he saith unto them, Whosoever shall put away his wife, and marry another, committeth adultery against her.

And if a woman shall put away her husband, and be married to another, she committeth adultery [Mark 10:10-12].

This is the strongest statement against divorce that is found in the Scripture. How is it to be interpreted? All the Scriptures on divorce should be brought together and considered before a proper induction can be made. The parallel passage in Matthew lists fornication as the one basis for divorce. Why did Mark omit this? Mark was writing to the Romans who did not know the Mosaic Law, while Matthew was writing for Israel who had and knew the Mosaic Law of divorce. So it must be considered in that light.

Romans 7:2 does not apply to the problem of divorce: "For the woman which hath an husband is bound by the law to her husband so long as he liveth; but if the husband be dead, she is loosed from the law of her husband." In this passage Paul is using a well-established law that a wife is bound to a living husband until death frees her as an illustration of the believer's relationship to the principle of law. The Mosaic system took care of the unfaithful wife or husband. They were stoned to death according to Deuteronomy 22:22-24. Now today we don't stone them to death. If we did, there would be so many rock piles we wouldn't be able to get around them.

According to the Mosaic Law, a husband or wife who is guilty of adultery may be treated as dead by the other mate. Scripture does recognize one ground for divorce — unfaithfulness. The innocent party is free to marry, it would seem, from Christ's words.

The discussion of divorce and the blessing of the little children are brought together by both Matthew and Mark. It seems to me the Spirit of God is trying to tell us something here. The child is the innocent product of the marriage, and a divorce becomes doubly evil because the little children suffer so in the divorce. It is amazing to see the number of young people from broken homes who get into trouble today. That is no accident, by any means. That is the way it works out.

And they brought young children to him, that he should touch them: and his disciples rebuked those that brought them.

But when Jesus saw it, he was much displeased, and said unto them, Suffer the little children to come unto me, and forbid them not: for of such is the kingdom of God.

Verily I say unto you, Whosoever shall not receive the kingdom of God as a little child, he shall not enter therein.

And he took them up in his arms, put his hands upon them, and blessed them [Mark 10:13-16].

The children would not have to become adults to come to Him. We wait for little Willie to grow up and maybe then he'll make a decision for Christ. Our Lord says that He wishes the adults would become little children. We hear so much today about going on and growing and developing. That's wonderful — after you have become a child of God. But, actually, most of us are going the wrong way. We need to leave our cleverness and our sophistication and our great knowledge that we boast of today, and return to the simplicity of childhood — with simple, childlike faith, trust Christ Jesus.

Our Lord took the children up in His arms, put His hands upon them, and blessed them. He never did take anybody else up in His arms like that, friend. He took the little children, because they are the ones He will receive. When they die in infancy, before the age of accountability, they go to be with Him.

And when he was gone forth into the way, there came one running, and kneeled to him, and asked him, Good Master, what shall I do that I may inherit eternal life?

And Jesus said unto him, Why callest thou me good? there is none good but one, that is, God [Mark 10:17,18].

In this day of crass materialism, this incident of the rich young ruler and the teaching of our Lord about riches are certainly very applicable. Matthew tells us that the ruler was young, and this was a normal question for a man under the Law to ask. He is living under the Mosaic system and is asking what he must do to inherit eternal life.

Jesus tries to get the young man to think. Why should he call Jesus *good*? There is only One who is good and that is God. If he is calling Jesus good, then Jesus is God. Now notice that Jesus gives the young man the commandments which are in the second section of the Ten Commandments.

> **Thou knowest the commandments, Do not commit adultery, Do not kill, Do not steal. Do not bear false witness, Defraud not, Honour thy father and mother.**
>
> **And he answered and said unto him, Master, all these have I observed from my youth [Mark 10:19,20].**

The first section of the commandments is labeled *pietas* and has to do with man's relationship to God. The second section is labeled *probitas* and has to do with man's relationship with man. Our Lord did not speak of the man's relationship to God but of his relationship to man. He could meet the standard of the second section and said he had kept them all.

> **Then Jesus beholding him loved him, and said unto him, One thing thou lackest: go thy way, sell whatsoever thou hast, and give to the poor, and thou shalt have treasure in heaven: and come, take up the cross, and follow me.**
>
> **And he was sad at that saying, and went away grieved: for he had great possessions [Mark 10:21,22].**

Jesus told him he lacked one thing. What was that? It was his relationship to God. The thing that was hindering him was his riches. He had called Jesus good, and if he will follow Jesus, he'll find out that the reason Jesus is good is because He is God. Jesus asked him to separate himself from his riches and follow Him. Where would this lead him? Well, at this time the Lord Jesus is on the way to die for the sins of this man. Had he followed Jesus, he would have come to the cross for redemption. But the young man "was sad at that saying, and went away grieved, for he had great possessions."

There is a great message here. Paul says that the love of money is a root of all evil (I Timothy 6:10). He was merely repeating what our Lord said in this discourse. Money will buy anything except the most valuable thing — eternal life. This discourse reveals the impossibility of a rich man to enter into heaven by means of his riches. It is impossible for any man to enter heaven by his own means.

> **And Jesus looked round about, and saith unto his disciples, How hardly shall they that have riches enter into the kingdom of God!**
>
> **And the disciples were astonished at his words. But Jesus answereth again, and saith unto them, Children, how hard is it for them that trust in riches to enter into the kingdom of God!**
>
> **It is easier for a camel to go through the eye of a needle, than for a rich man to enter into the kingdom of God [Mark 10:23-25].**

Well, a camel can't go through the eye of a needle. That's humanly impossible, or should we say "camel" impossible. But for God all things are possible.

> **And they were astonished out of measure, saying among themselves, Who then can be saved?**
>
> **And Jesus looking upon them saith, With men it is impossible, but not with God: for with God all things are possible [Mark 10:26,27].**

The man can't do it; only the Lord Jesus can. We have the idea today that money can buy everything. Someone has written these lines about money that we do well to think over:

Money will buy a bed, but it will not buy sleep.
Money will buy food, but it will not buy an appetite.
Money will buy medicine, but it will not buy health.
Money will buy a house, but it will not buy a home.
Money will buy a diamond, but it will not buy love.
Money will buy a church pew, but it will not buy
    salvation.

Jesus invited this young man to get rid of that which stood between him and God. If he had followed the Lord Jesus, he would have learned that the reason Jesus is good is because Jesus is God.

> **Then Peter began to say unto him, Lo, we have left all, and have followed thee.**
>
> **And Jesus answered and said, Verily I say unto you, There is no man that hath left house, or brethren, or sisters, or father, or mother, or wife, or children, or lands, for my sake, and the gospel's,**
>
> **But he shall receive an hundredfold now in this time, houses, and brethren, and sisters, and mothers, and children, and lands, with persecutions; and in the world to come eternal life [Mark 10:28-30].**

Instead of rebuking Peter, Jesus promised a reward for those who sacrifice for Him.

> **But many that are first shall be last; and the last first [Mark 10:31].**

This is a principle which will operate in giving out rewards.

> **And they were in the way going up to Jerusalem; and Jesus went before them: and they were amazed; and as they followed, they were afraid. And he took again the twelve, and began to tell them what things should happen unto him,**
>
> **Saying, Behold, we go up to Jerusalem; and the Son of man shall be delivered unto the chief priests, and unto the scribes; and they shall condemn him to death, and shall deliver him to the Gentiles:**
>
> **And they shall mock him, and shall scourge him, and shall spit upon him, and shall kill him: and the third day he shall rise again [Mark 10:32-34].**

You see, He's moving now toward Jerusalem. He knows and He is telling them that He is going there to die. Notice again that with His death, He always mentions His resurrection.

> **And James and John, the sons of Zebedee, come unto**

him, saying, Master, we would that thou shouldest do for us whatsoever we shall desire.

And he said unto them, What would ye that I should do for you?

They said unto him, Grant unto us that we may sit, one on the right hand, and the other on thy left hand, in thy glory.

But Jesus said unto them, Ye know not what ye ask: can ye drink of the cup that I drink of? and be baptized with the baptism that I am baptized with? [Mark 10:35-38].

We had this story in Matthew, you will remember. The mother had come to Jesus and asked this privilege for her sons. So when Jesus asked them whether they could be baptized with the same baptism that He would suffer, they answered that they could.

And they said unto him, We can. And Jesus said unto them, Ye shall indeed drink of the cup that I drink of; and with the baptism that I am baptized withal shall ye be baptized:

But to sit on my right hand and on my left hand is not mine to give; but it shall be given to them for whom it is prepared [Mark 10:39,40].

We know that James became a martyr. John was exiled on the Isle of Patmos. Although it is not believed that he was martyred, he may have been executed; we do not know.

Our Lord did not say that there is not a place on His right hand and left hand. He said the place is not given arbitrarily to anyone He wants to give it to. But those who will receive it are preparing themselves for that place. Friends, you get heaven as a gift. But your place in heaven — you work for that. Salvation is free, but we work for a reward. If you are going to be rewarded of Him, you won't get it by twiddling your thumbs or wringing your hands or sitting in a rocking chair. You'll have to work to receive that.

And when the ten heard it, they began to be much displeased with James and John [Mark 10:41].

They were displeased because *they* wanted the best positions.

So the Lord must teach them another principle. The method
this world uses is not God's method.

> But Jesus called them to him, and saith unto them, Ye
> know that they which are accounted to rule over the
> Gentiles exercise lordship over them; and their great
> ones exercise authority upon them.

> But so shall it not be among you: but whosoever will be
> great among you, shall be your minister.

> And whosoever of you will be the chiefest, shall be ser-
> vant of all [Mark 10:42-44].

God's method is to take those who are humble and make
themselves small by serving, and place them as the leaders. The
chief must be the servant of all. Then He states the key to this
Gospel:

> For even the Son of man came not to be ministered unto,
> but to minister, and to give his life a ransom for many
> [Mark 10:45].

This account appears in Matthew and again in Luke. There
are people who deny the inerrancy of Scripture because they
can't reconcile the accounts of the Gospels here. Matthew mentions two blind men but Mark centers his attention on Bartimaeus because he was the one who spoke out. I think the critic
who tries to tear apart the accounts in the Gospels is the third
blind man!

> And they came to Jericho: and as he went out of Jericho
> with his disciples and a great number of people, blind
> Bartimaeus, the son of Timaeus, sat by the highway side
> begging.

> And when he heard that it was Jesus of Nazareth, he
> began to cry out, and say, Jesus, thou son of David, have
> mercy on me.

> And many charged him that he should hold his peace:
> but he cried the more a great deal, Thou son of David,
> have mercy on me.

> And Jesus stood still, and commanded him to be called.

And they call the blind man, saying unto him, Be of good comfort, rise; he calleth thee.

And he, casting away his garment, rose, and came to Jesus.

And Jesus answered and said unto him, What wilt thou that I should do unto thee? The blind man said unto him, Lord, that I might receive my sight.

And Jesus said unto him, Go thy way; thy faith hath made thee whole. And immediately he received his sight, and followed Jesus in the way [Mark 10:46-52].

It is thrilling to think that Bartimaeus followed Jesus now with his eyes open. In a few days he will see Jesus dying on the cross.

Are you blind? Or have you, too, seen Jesus dying for you? Look and Live!

CHAPTER 11

We are coming now to the last days in the earthly life of our Lord. I have divided this chapter in this way:

1. Jesus presents Himself publicly to his nation as the Messiah (vv. 1-11).

2. Jesus pronounces a blight on the fig tree (vv. 12-14).

3. Jesus purifies the temple (vv. 15-21).

4. Jesus' prayer discourse (vv. 22-26).

5. Jesus perturbs the religious rulers (vv. 27-33).

This eleventh chapter deals with the three days that He came in to Jerusalem. I take the position that His so-called triumphal entry really wasn't that at all. It was the Lord Jesus coming to Jerusalem in a public manner at the conclusion of His earthly ministry and presenting Himself. Actually, it amounted to a rejection of His overture. He really came in on three separate days, and not on just one day. I think that each Gospel is presenting a different aspect of His coming into Jerusalem. The first day He came was a Sabbath day, Saturday. He returned on Sunday and cleansed the temple. Then He returned on Monday and wept over the city.

> **And when they came nigh to Jerusalem, unto Bethphage and Bethany, at the mount of Olives, he sendeth forth two of his disciples [Mark 11:1].**

We have seen in the last few chapters that Jesus was moving toward Jerusalem. He's moving geographically and He's moving chronologically closer to His death. This is the last week of His earthly life. Bethany and Bethphage are two little towns on the other side of the Mount of Olives from Jerusalem. (I intended to walk over there and back myself, but I never got around to it the few days that I was in Jerusalem. If I ever go there again, I want to do that. The fact of the matter is that I want to spend more time walking through that land. It's one thing to get in a bus or a

car and ride along and have these places pointed out, but it's
another thing to take a map and walk along, stopping along the
way and having a conversation with anyone who could understand English. I know one could discover many things which the
average tourist does not see at all today.)

Now the Lord Jesus is giving directions to two of His men.

> **And saith unto them, Go your way into the village over
> against you: and as soon as ye be entered into it, ye shall
> find a colt tied, whereon never man sat; loose him, and
> bring him.**
>
> **And if any may say unto you, Why do ye this? say ye that
> the Lord hath need of him; and straightway he will send
> him hither [Mark 11:2,3].**

There are two possible explanations regarding the colt that
Jesus was to ride into Jerusalem. The Lord Jesus could have
known about it since He is God and, therefore, omniscient. This
could have been a miracle from beginning to end. On the other
hand, all of this could have been arranged beforehand, and it
would therefore be entirely human. It doesn't seem necessary to
read a miracle in here when the natural explanation is in order. I
believe our Lord had arranged for this beforehand, and I think
you will find greater meaning if you look at it that way. The important feature is that Jesus is asserting His authority. Notice
that if anyone questions them about loosing the colt, they are to
say that the Lord has need of it. That is asserting authority.

While some are plotting His death, others are yielding
allegiance to Him. "Straightway he will send him hither." There
were those who were obeying Him. Now that has been true for
over 1900 years. There are these two classes of people even today.
As we read on, we find that they went into the town and found
things just as the Lord had said.

> **And they went their way, and found the colt tied by the
> door without in a place where two ways met; and they
> loose him.**
>
> **And certain of them that stood there said unto them,
> What do ye, loosing the colt?**

**And they said unto them even as Jesus had commanded:
and they let them go [Mark 11:4-6].**

You will notice that they merely follow His instructions and
return with the colt.

**And they brought the colt to Jesus, and cast their gar-
ments on him; and he sat upon him.**

**And many spread their garments in the way: and others
cut down branches off the trees, and strawed them in the
way.**

**And they that went before, and they that followed, cried,
saying, Hosanna; Blessed is he that cometh in the name
of the Lord [Mark 11:7-9].**

I'm not sure that this was very impressive to those in
Jerusalem. I'm sure it would not have been impressive to anyone
who had been in Rome at the time that one of the Caesars
returned from a campaign and had a great triumphal entry, a
victorious return of a Caesar. It is said that so much booty and so
many captives were brought back that the parade would go on
for two or three days and nights. That would be triumphal, you
see.

Here it was just a few Galileans, peasants, but the impressive
thing and the important thing is that the Lord Jesus is offering
Himself publicly.

**And Jesus entered into Jerusalem, and into the temple:
and when he had looked round about upon all things,
and now the eventide was come, he went out unto
Bethany with the twelve [Mark 11:11].**

There are two things here that are important to see. It was obviously the Sabbath day and the money changers and the oxen
were not there. On this first day He came in as the Priest, and He
was the sacrifice. He came in as the great High Priest to offer the
sacrifice that is acceptable to God for your sins and for my sins.

And note that He did not spend the night in Jerusalem but
returned to Bethany for the evening. Jesus had thrust Himself
before the city publicly and was demanding a decision. As far as

we can tell, He did not spend a night in the city that rejected
Him.

**And on the morrow, when they were come from Bethany,
he was hungry:**

**And seeing a fig tree afar off having leaves, he came, if
haply he might find any thing thereon: and when he
came to it, he found nothing but leaves; for the time of
figs was not yet.**

**And Jesus answered and said unto it, No man eat fruit of
thee hereafter for ever. And his disciples heard it [Mark
11:12-14].**

And this is "on the morrow," the second day, and they were
coming from Bethany. This is the second day He entered in
triumph. This little incident has caused great controversy. On
this day He cleansed the temple and He cursed the fig tree.

The nation Israel, in my opinion, is represented by the fig tree.
I recognize there are others who will take exception to that, and I
don't want to be controversial. What I'm interested in is that
there is a great spiritual lesson here. They had the outward leaves
of a God-given religion, but there was no spiritual fruit. I wonder
if we could say that of the church today? This would be His
message to the church of Laodicea. They didn't have anything —
they were poor and blind and needed to have ointment to open
their eyes. This means that the Holy Spirit was not there. I
believe this is the same thing that Isaiah was talking about in
Isaiah 29:13: "Wherefore the Lord said, Forasmuch as this
people draw near me with their mouth, and with their lips do
honour me, but have removed their heart far from me, and their
fear toward me is taught by the precept of man." I would con-
sider this the condition of the church today.

The Lord Jesus cursed the fig tree, and the fig tree withered
away.

**And they come to Jerusalem: and Jesus went into the
temple, and began to cast out them that sold and bought
in the temple, and overthrew the tables of the money-
changers, and the seats of them that sold doves [Mark
11:15].**

Here He cleanses the temple. John tells us that He cleansed it at the beginning of His ministry and now He cleanses it at the end of His ministry. This took place on the second day, and this was not the Sabbath day, but it was Sunday. The money-changers were now in the temple. They had a seat on the stock market and were there so that when strangers came from other countries they could exchange coins. The strangers couldn't use their foreign coins but needed the legal coin of the temple. When these money-changers would make the exchange, they, of course, charged the people a certain percentage. It served a good purpose in a way, but the trouble of it was that our Lord said it had become a den of thieves. It had become a religious racket.

Friends, this is always a danger in any Christian enterprise. That is the reason folks ought to check on religious organizations before they support them.

You see, His public presentation of Himself as the Messiah was not a triumphal entry into Jerusalem. He was *rejected*. I don't like the term, and it is not scriptural to call it "triumphal." Wait until you see Him someday when He comes and the "dead in Christ shall rise first and then we which are alive and remain shall be caught up together with them" (I Thessalonians 4:16, 17). You will see that tremendous throng of folk who have trusted Christ during 1900 years or more — millions of saints going out. My friends, that will really be a triumphal entry. I think it's going to take place over a long period of time. The raising will be in a moment, in the twinkling of an eye, but the parade has a long way to go. He's going to lead them into a new place, a new creation, a new home for this new group. It will not be just to the moon, but to the New Jerusalem. What a glorious thing that will be! That will be triumphant!

We have come now to the third day.

And in the morning, as they passed by, they saw the fig tree dried up from the roots.

And Peter calling to remembrance saith unto him, Master, behold, the fig tree which thou cursedst is withered away [Mark 11:20,21].

This causes our Lord to give this discourse on prayer. They

marvelled at the fig tree, and this causes Him to give the discourse.

And Jesus answering saith unto them, Have faith in God [Mark 11:22].

It's interesting that this discourse on the prayer of faith grew out of Peter's calling attention to the blighted fig tree. You see, the first step in prayer must be faith in God. The writer to the Hebrews stated this same principle: "But without faith it is impossible to please him: for he that cometh to God must believe that he is, and that he is a rewarder of them that diligently seek him" (Hebrews 11:6).

If you don't believe in God, friends, then the skeptic is certainly correct when he says that prayer is a madman talking to himself. Having faith in God is the first step.

For verily I say unto you, That whosoever shall say unto this mountain, Be thou removed, and be thou cast into the sea; and shall not doubt in his heart, but shall believe that those things which he saith shall come to pass; he shall have whatsoever he saith [Mark 11:23].

This is a verse that is so misunderstood today. The Christian does not need to throw mountains around literally, but he needs power for living and meeting the daily mountains of cares and problems. This is why Paul could pray for the Ephesians, "That he would grant you, according to the riches of his glory, to be strengthened with might by his Spirit in the inner man" (Ephesians 3:16). Don't pray for me that I'll be able to move the mountains that are behind our headquarters up here in Pasadena. Frankly, I see no point in moving the mountains. And if I did move them, where in the world would I move them? I don't want to put them out in the ocean because they look pretty up where they are. But I want to tell you very candidly that I would like to be strengthened with might by the Holy Spirit in the inner man. That, my friend, would be greater than moving a mountain. That's the thing that is important and is, I feel, what He is talking about as He gives them this visible illustration to show what prayer can do.

Therefore I say unto you, What things soever ye desire,

when ye pray, believe that ye receive them, and ye shall have them [Mark 11:24].

Have faith in God. This does not give you the ability to satisfy your own selfish desires, but have faith in God that His will might be done in your life.

And when ye stand praying, forgive, if ye have ought against any: that your Father also which is in heaven may forgive you your trespasses.

But if ye do not forgive, neither will your Father which is in heaven forgive your trespasses [Mark 11:25,26].

Here is a condition that the individual must meet before prayer is heard and answered. An unforgiving spirit will short circuit the power of prayer and that's important. God forgives us for Christ's sake (Ephesians 4:32). That is the way we are saved. But if you and I are going to have power in our lives, there must be forgiveness. That is very important.

Now we find the chief priests coming out to try to trap Him.

And they come again to Jerusalem: and as he was walking in the temple, there come to him the chief priests, and the scribes, and the elders,

And say unto him, By what authority doest thou these things? and who gave thee this authority to do these things? [Mark 11:27,28].

They are still on His trail, you see, these bloodhounds of hate. They are resisting Him at every turn. They challenged His authority. They were the religious rulers, they were the official representatives of religion in their day, and they had delegated no authority to Him. So they want to know where He got His authority.

And Jesus answered and said unto them, I will also ask of you one question, and answer me, and I will tell you by what authority I do these things.

The baptism of John, was it from heaven, or of men? answer me [Mark 11:29,30].

That was a good question, by the way, and it was a devastating question to the religious rulers. You see, if they said that John's baptism was from heaven, then the obvious follow-up would be, "Then why didn't you accept it?" If they repudiated John, then the people would be antagonized, for they accepted John.

> **And they reasoned with themselves, saying, If we shall say, From heaven; he will say, Why then did ye not believe him?**
>
> **But if we shall say, Of men; they feared the people: for all men counted John, that he was a prophet indeed.**
>
> **And they answered and said unto Jesus, We cannot tell. And Jesus answering saith unto them, Neither do I tell you by what authority I do these things [Mark 11:31-33].**

They had to wiggle out of answering the question of Jesus by claiming ignorance. It might be argued that this did not afford Jesus a sufficient ground for not answering their question. My friend, they were not seeking an answer. They were trying to trap Him. They had no intention of following His teaching if He had told them. He does not answer them because He is not falling into their trap. This, to me, is one of the great proofs of His deity — the way He handled His enemies.

Remember that when men and women came to our Lord with sincere questions as sincere seekers, they received a sincere and genuine answer to their inquiries.

CHAPTER 12

Note in this chapter and in succeeding chapters that there are no miracles. We have stated before that Mark is the Gospel of action with the emphasis on miracles. According to this premise, it would seem that the action is slowing down now to a standstill. Actually, this is the lull before the storm. And we'll still see a lot of action coming up.

Now I've made a little outline of this chapter that I'll give you:

1. Jesus quickens the battle with the religious rulers with the parable of the vineyard (vv. 1-12).

2. Jesus queers the plot of the Pharisees and Herodians about paying taxes to Caesar (vv. 13-17).

3. Jesus quells the skepticism of the Sadducees concerning the resurrection (vv. 18-27).

4. Jesus quiets the mind of the scribe about the greatest commandment (vv. 28-34).

5. Jesus questions the Pharisees about the Messiah and quotes Psalm 110 (vv. 35-40).

6. Jesus qualifies scriptural giving by evaluating the two mites of the widow (vv. 41-44).

We are coming to a great deal of action but a different kind. The Lord Jesus is the Passover Lamb and He is put up for close inspection now before He is to be slaughtered. (You remember that the Passover lamb was kept up and closely observed to make sure it was without blemish.) All the waves of men's wrath will roll over His head in a few days now. This is not a period of quiet and inaction, but the fiercest encounter with the religious rulers. Both sides bring up their heavy artillery and make every arrangement and preparation for the battle of heaven and hell, light and darkness, God and Satan. This could hardly be called a period of inaction or cessation of hostilities.

The three years of periodic skirmishes of Jesus with the religious rulers breaks out in a bitter verbal encounter. He takes the initiative, wins a victory in the verbal area, and they cease trying to trap Him in that way. They had hoped to force Him to say something that would turn the people against Him. All the questions they asked Him were loaded.

He precipitated this action by giving the most pointed, plain, and direct parable of His ministry — the Vineyard. The meaning is obvious. The chapter opens with this parable.

And he began to speak unto them by parables. A certain man planted a vineyard, and set an hedge about it, and digged a place for the winefat, and built a tower, and let it out to husbandmen, and went into a far country [Mark 12:1].

The vineyard is the nation Israel according to Isaiah 5:1-7. He brought that "vine" out of Egypt; He planted it (the nation of Israel). He gave to them a God-given religion. They are the only people that ever had a God-given religion and the visible presence of God. Churches have never had that. Now He gives a parable for the religious rulers of His day.

And at the season he sent to the husbandmen a servant, that he might receive from the husbandmen of the fruit of the vineyard.

And they caught him, and beat him, and sent him away empty.

And again he sent unto them another servant; and at him they cast stones, and wounded him in the head, and sent him away shamefully handled.

And again he sent another; and him they killed, and many others; beating some, and killing some. Having yet therefore one son, his wellbeloved, he sent him also last unto them, saying, They will reverence my son.

But those husbandmen said among themselves, This is the heir; come, let us kill him, and the inheritance shall be our's.

And they took him, and killed him, and cast him out of the vineyard.

What shall therefore the lord of the vineyard do? he will come and destroy the husbandmen, and will give the vineyard unto others.

And have ye not read this scripture: The stone which the builders rejected is become the head of the corner:

This was the Lord's doing, and it is marvellous in our eyes?

And they sought to lay hold on him, but feared the people: for they knew that he had spoken the parable against them: and they left him, and went their way [Mark 12:2-12].

It is quite obvious what He is talking about in this parable. The servants that God sent were the prophets. The "certain man" who had the vineyard is God the Father. The vineyard is the nation Israel. God had chosen and protected this nation. The husbandmen were the religious rulers. Finally, He sent His Son and that, of course, is the Lord Jesus, the beloved Son of the Father. In a special way, Jesus came to the nation Israel first. "I am not sent but unto the lost sheep of the house of Israel" (Matthew 15:24). But He also did come for the entire world according to John 3:16. But here our Lord is making a deliberate and direct thrust at the religious rulers who stood before Him. They had already plotted His death and He brings their plans out into the light. "He knew what was in man." He tells the religious rulers what they will do. He prophesied their every step and anticipated their every move. He charges them with murder before they kill Him. This is a remarkable incident, friends. Then He predicts the judgment of the religious rulers. We can see the fulfillment of that in A.D. 70 when Titus the Roman destroyed that city and took them into captivity. We can go look at the Colosseum at Rome. It was Jewish slave labor that built it.

Now let us notice something wonderful here. "The stone which the builders rejected is become the head of the corner." This is like a two-in-one parable of the vineyard and the stone. Christ was a stumbling stone and a rock of offence to the religious

rulers, but many of the people turned to Him and He became
the headstone of the corner. This will ultimately be fulfilled in
the future when He comes again to the earth. We find this
described in Zechariah 4:7: "Who art thou, O great mountain?
before Zerubbabel thou shalt become a plain: and he shall bring
forth the headstone thereof with shoutings, crying, Grace, grace
unto it."

The religious rulers would have taken the Lord Jesus at this
time and executed Him, but they were afraid of the people, you
see. This parable of the vineyard set off a verbal war, and they
send further delegations to Him.

> **And they send unto him certain of the Pharisees and of
> the Herodians, to catch him in his words.**

> **And when they were come, they say unto him, Master,
> we know that thou art true, and carest for no man: for
> thou regardest not the person of men, but teachest the
> way of God in truth: Is it lawful to give tribute to Caesar,
> or not?**

> **Shall we give, or shall we not give? But he, knowing their
> hypocrisy, said unto them, Why tempt ye me? bring me a
> penny, that I may see it [Mark 12:13-15].**

Their question is a masterpiece. They flattered Him but He
called them hypocrites. He didn't accept their flattery. (By the
way, He did accept what Nicodemus had said to Him because he
was sincere.) My, but they were hypocrites!

Why did He ask them for a penny? He is going to use their own
coin, it is true, but I think that He didn't have one Himself. Just
think of that. The Lord of Glory is in this world and He didn't
have a dime in His pocket, friends. Can you imagine that? How
wonderful He was! He didn't have a coin and He didn't have a
lot of credit cards in His pocket either. So He just asked them for
a coin and they gave Him one.

> **And they brought it. And he saith unto them, Whose is
> this image and superscription? And they said unto him,
> Caesar's.**

> **And Jesus answering said unto them, Render to Caesar**

**the things that are Caesar's, and to God the things that
are God's. And they marvelled at him. [Mark 12:16,17].**

They gave Him a coin, and He asked them the question. You
see, if He had answered them that they are to pay tribute to
Caesar, then that would have meant that He put Caesar ahead of
Moses and ahead of the Messiah. And if He said they were not to
pay tribute, He would have been guilty of insurrection against
Caesar. They thought they had Him in a trap, but they didn't
have Him at all. They had to marvel at His answer.

His answer reveals that a child of God has a two-fold responsibility and, in fact, maybe even more than two-fold. Someone
told me some time ago that his father was in the hospital and his
mother was sick but that he had some money set aside as a
church contribution. When I inquired further, he said his parents
were really in dire need and would have to accept charity if he
didn't help them. So I told him that his responsibility was to
them. We get some strange, pious, notions today.

We do have a responsibility to our government. When I see my
income tax, sometimes I think I have too much responsibility. It
pinches and hurts me when I see the way some of our senators are
living and when I see the corruption that is taking place in all
areas of government today. I must confess that then I resent paying the income tax. But that does not mean that I ought not to
pay some. We have a definite responsibility to government.

Also we have a responsibility to our loved ones. We have a
responsibility to our church. I have a responsibility to you, today,
to give the Word of God to you. We all have our responsibilities,
and that is what the Lord is saying. You have a responsibility to
Caesar. Discharge it. But that doesn't relieve you of your responsibility to God. My, what a marvellous incident!

Actually, He takes this incident and turns it into a parable.
"Give Me a coin." With that coin, He illustrated a great truth.
The coin has two sides. There are two areas of life in which we
have a responsibility. Man has both an earthly or physical and a
heavenly or spiritual obligation. Citizens of heaven pay taxes
down here. Pilgrims down here should deposit eternal wealth in
heaven. So you see how He silenced these Herodians who wanted
to put the house of Herod into power.

> **Then come unto him the Sadducees, which say there is no resurrection; and they asked him, saying,**
>
> **Master, Moses wrote unto us, If a man's brother die, and leave his wife behind him, and leave no children, that his brother should take his wife, and raise up seed unto his brother [Mark 12:18,19].**

The Sadducees, you will remember, were the liberals of the day. They denied the supernatural. What they stated was accurate, by the way. They referred to the law of the kinsman redeemer which is illustrated in the Book of Ruth. They knew what the Scripture said.

> **Now there were seven brethren: and the first took a wife, and dying left no seed.**
>
> **And the second took her, and died, neither left he any seed: and the third likewise.**
>
> **And the seven had her, and left no seed: last of all the woman died also [Mark 12:20-22].**

This is a ridiculous illustration, isn't it? Well, it could be duplicated today in Hollywood or in our contemporary society perhaps, but it is ridiculous. So their question is:

> **In the resurrection therefore, when they shall rise, whose wife shall she be of them? for the seven had her to wife.**
>
> **And Jesus answering said unto them, Do ye not therefore err, because ye know not the scriptures, neither the power of God? [Mark 12:23,24].**

I would say that this is the difficulty today with those who are so critical of the Scriptures — they do not know the Scriptures nor the power of God. I notice that right now there is a promotion to cut down the population explosion and some folk say this is contrary to the Bible. God said to Adam, "Be fruitful and multiply." It is true that God did say that to Adam but He didn't say that to the "Adamses" today. He wasn't talking to this present generation. If you and your wife were the only couple on earth. I imagine that is what He would say to you. He did repeat it again to Noah when Noah was very much alone with his family and there was no one else on earth. But He didn't repeat that for us today. This is not even stated for Christians to do. It shows a woeful ignorance of the Bible, and yet today such people spout off about the Bible when they should not be heard.

The Lord told the Sadducees that they were ignorant of two things:

1. They did not know the Scriptures.

2. They did not know the power of God.

For when they shall rise from the dead, they neither marry, nor are given in marriage; but are as the angels which are in heaven [Mark 12:25].

This doesn't mean that a man and a woman who were together down here can't be together in heaven. They won't be together as man and wife. They are not establishing a home up there nor are they raising children. That's the thing that He's saying to them here.

And as touching the dead, that they rise: have ye not read in the book of Moses, how in the bush God spake unto him, saying, I am the God of Abraham, and the God of Isaac, and the God of Jacob?

He is not the God of the dead, but the God of the living: ye therefore do greatly err [Mark 12:26,27].

They do not know the power of God. Moses is not dead; Abraham is not dead; Isaac is not dead. Their bodies were buried there in Hebron but they are not dead. They have gone to be with Him and that is where the Christians are today that die in the Lord, friends. He is devastating in His answers to these religious rulers. Now we have another person coming to our Lord, after hearing the discussion with the Sadducees.

And one of the scribes came, and having heard them reasoning together, and perceiving that he had answered them well, asked him, Which is the first commandment of all?

And Jesus answered him, The first of all the com-

mandments is, Hear, O Israel; The Lord our God is one Lord [Mark 12:28,29].

This is a quotation from Deuteronomy 6:4. It is not one of the Ten Commandments, but it is the greatest doctrinal statement in the Old Testament. Literally it should read, "Jehovah our Elohim [plural] is one Jehovah." Israel was to witness to a world of polytheism and idolatry concerning the unity of the Godhead. The church is to witness to a world of atheism and unitarianism concerning the Trinity.

And thou shalt love the Lord thy God with all thy heart, and with all thy soul, and with all thy mind, and with all thy strength: this is the first commandment [Mark 12:30].

By the way, do you keep this commandment, my friend? If you say that you don't need Christ as a Saviour, that you obey God, then I ask you this question, "Do you love God with all your heart and mind and soul?" If you don't, then you are breaking His commandment and you need a Saviour. I *know* I need a Saviour. I don't measure up here. I wish I did. I love Him, but not as I should.

And the second is like, namely this, Thou shalt love thy neighbor as thyself. There is none other commandment greater than these [Mark 12:31].

Now, if you can measure up here, maybe you could apply for salvation on your own merit. Until you do, you need a Saviour.

And the scribe said unto him, Well, Master, thou hast said the truth: for there is one God; and there is none other but he:

And to love him with all the heart, and with all the understanding, and with all the soul, and with all the strength, and to love his neighbour as himself, is more than all whole burnt-offerings and sacrifices.

And when Jesus saw that he answered discreetly, he said unto him, Thou art not far from the kingdom of God. And no man after that durst ask him any question [Mark 12:32-34].

What the scribe said is certainly true. To love God and to love our neighbor is more than all offerings and sacrifices. Friend, may I say again, if you don't measure up to loving God with all your heart and understanding and soul and strength and to loving your neighbor as yourself, then you need a Saviour. Turn to Him! Now this ended the question period as far as men asking Jesus questions was concerned. The enemy could not trap Him. Now Jesus is going to do the questioning.

> And Jesus answered and said, while he taught in the temple, How say the scribes that Christ is the son of David?
>
> For David himself said by the Holy Ghost, The Lord said to my Lord, Sit thou on my right hand, till I make thine enemies thy footstool.
>
> David therefore himself calleth him Lord; and whence is he then his son? And the common people heard him gladly [Mark 12:35-37].

Right here Jesus is teaching His own virgin birth. How could David, in Psalm 110 where he is speaking of a future descendant of his, call his own great-great-great-great-grandson his Lord? Well, the only way he can call Him his Lord is for Him to be The LORD, friends. The only way He can be The LORD is to be more than David's son. He must be virgin born to be the Son of God. This is a great thought that our Lord is teaching here.

Notice also that here Jesus definitely ascribes Psalm 110 to David. He says that David wrote this Psalm by the Holy Spirit. And Jesus says that this Psalm is speaking concerning Him, the Messiah.

> And he said unto them in his doctrine, Beware of the scribes, which love to go in long clothing, and love salutations in the market-places,
>
> And the chief seats in the synagogues, and the uppermost rooms at feasts:
>
> Which devour widows' houses, and for a pretence make long prayers: these shall receive greater damnation [Mark 12:38-40].

Jesus is teaching that privilege creates responsibility. He denounces the scribes because their lives contradicted the Scriptures they taught. Their judgment will be more severe than those who have not heard the Scriptures.

The final incident in this chapter shows Jesus doing an audacious thing that only God should do. He watched how the people gave.

> **And Jesus sat over against the treasury, and beheld how the people cast money into the treasury: and many that were rich cast in much [Mark 12:41].**

He has the authority today to stand over the taking of the offering in your church or whenever you are asked to give to some cause; that is, for God's work. He's there to watch you, friends. He doesn't watch what you give. He watches how much you keep for yourself.

> **And there came a certain poor widow, and she threw in two mites, which make a farthing [Mark 12:42].**

He had noted that the rich cast in much. They were the big givers. Oh my, how we love the big givers. The rich gave generously. But He didn't commend that. He watched that widow, and she gave two mites. Compared to the wealth of that temple, friends, what she gave wasn't worth a snap of your fingers. But do you know what He did? He took those two mites and He just kissed them into the coin and the gold of heaven, and made them more valuable than anything any rich man ever gave. Do you know why? Because He saw that she kept nothing for herself but gave all to Him. Her love and devotion were in the gift. I tell you, that is the way He measures.

Some folk ask whether they should give a tenth to God. My friend, how much do you keep for yourself? It's not how much you give to Him. You're not required to give a certain amount or a certain percentage. The question is, how much do you really love Him? The Lord is the One who watches how people give. It's not what they put in. The widow didn't give anything of great value, friends. I doubt that the treasurer paid much attention to it. But the Lord takes the two coppers of the widow and exchanges them for the gold of heaven.

CHAPTER 13

Again in this chapter we will find that there are no miracles but there is a great deal of action. Mark's Gospel is a Gospel of action and has placed much emphasis on miracles. But in this chapter the action is *future* action. The action really hasn't come to a standstill but it is still future. It records the eschatological events which will end this age. The catastrophic events of the Great Tribulation are given, and the Second Coming of Christ is graphically described. This is action geared to the divine power and that, my friend, is greater than atomic power.

The Olivet Discourse which we find in this chapter is a parallel account with Matthew. It is much briefer here than in Matthew; in fact, it is an abridged edition. This has been true of Mark all the way through, except in some notable instances where he gives the longest account of an incident. In general, his policy is to abbreviate everything and give rapid action.

This is my outline of the chapter:

1. Presentation of questions by disciples to Jesus on top of the Mount of Olives (vv. 1-4).

2. Panorama of this age (vv. 5-7).

3. Persecution preceding the Great Tribulation (vv. 8-13).

4. Prophecy of the Great Tribulation (vv. 14-23).

5. Proclamation of the Second Coming of Christ (vv. 24-27).

6. Parable of the fig tree (vv. 28-33).

7. Program for God's people (vv. 34-37).

There are a lot of "P's" in that pod, don't you think? That's what we have in this chapter before us.

And as he went out of the temple, one of his disciples saith unto him, Master, see what manner of stones and what buildings are here! [Mark 13:1].

Now here, I think, is an example of how there can be a mis-understanding of a passage of Scripture. One naturally asks the question, "What's back of all this?" We have no indication why the disciples should make such a statement. Actually, we must go back to Matthew 23:38 to find out. Jesus had pronounced a coming desolation upon the Temple. The disciples were puzzled because there was a grandeur and a glory about the Temple and the surrounding building. They wanted to be sure that He noted it. So they said, "Master, see what manner of stones and what buildings are here!"

And Jesus answering said unto him, Seest thou these great buildings? there shall not be left one stone upon another, that shall not be thrown down [Mark 13:2].

He asks them a question. They had asked Him to see the buildings because they wanted to make sure that He hadn't missed them. Now He asks them, "Do you really see them?"

Jesus is teaching a great spiritual lesson here. During the last few years of my pastorate in downtown Los Angeles, a forty-two story building went up right next door to the church. Across the way, within a block and a half is a forty-story building, two fifty-story buildings within a block of us, and diagonally across the street from us will be a sixty-story building. Down the street from us they plan the greatest downtown shopping area in America. There will be several skyscrapers, a big shopping mall, a great department store, two hotels. My friend, we could ask that question today. Don't you see all these beautiful buildings? They're brand new and they are beautiful. But what do we really see? We see their beauty, strength, stability, and permanence. It looks to me as if they are here for a long time unless a bad earthquake comes along. Really these buildings are temporary. They are passing away. A true perspective would allow us to see that not one stone is going to be left upon another. Actually, these are of steel and concrete, but still they are all coming down. Paul stated the spiritual truth this way: "While we look not at the things which are seen, but at the things which are not seen: for the things which are seen are temporal; but the things which are not seen are eternal" (II Corinthians 4:18).

My friend, that is the great truth. Did you know that Nebuchadnezzar walked through great Babylon in his day and saw all the glory of Babylon. As he walked through, he said, "Is not this great Babylon that I built?" Have you seen a picture of the ruins of Babylon today? Nothing to brag about there. It's all gone, friends, the glory has disappeared. And the skyscrapers of Los Angeles are all coming down, too, by the way. He says it will all come down. These things are passing away.

My friend, do you see the things that are eternal?

And as he sat upon the mount of Olives over against the temple, Peter and James and John and Andrew asked him privately,

Tell us, when shall these things be? and what shall be the sign when all these things shall be fulfilled? [Mark 13:3,4].

Mark is always putting in a little something that we don't get in the other Gospels. We wouldn't have known it was these four men who actually were delegated as the committee who waited on Him with the questions, but here they are. Remember, this is Peter's Gospel. Peter told Mark that these four men were in the group that asked Him privately.

Mark states two of the questions. Matthew states three questions that they asked. Luke gives part of the answer. When we put it all together we find that Matthew records all three questions put to our Lord by the disciples:

1. "Tell us when shall these things be?" This refers to when one stone will not be left on another. Luke gives our Lord's answer to this question.

2. What shall be the sign of Thy coming?

3. What shall be the sign of the end of the age?

Matthew and Mark give our Lord's answer to the last two questions. Matthew has it in a great deal more detail than Mark, but we will look at Mark's emphasis. Remember that he is writing to the Romans, and he is going to call attention to that which reveals power and action and drama.

And Jesus answering them began to say, Take heed lest any man deceive you:

**For many shall come in my name, saying, I am Christ;
and shall deceive many [Mark 13:5, 6].**

We find this is a constant warning — a warning against false
Christs. Some may think that this is not a danger today. I think
it is very pertinent right now. For example, the Christ of
liberalism is an antichrist — he is not the real Christ! Some of
you may think that they preach the Christ of the Bible. They do
not. According to their statements, the Christ they preach was
not virgin born, he never performed a miracle, did not shed his
blood for the sins of the world, was not raised bodily from the
grave, did not ascend into heaven, and is not coming again
bodily. Do you know there is no Jesus like that in the Bible? The
Jesus of the Bible was virgin born and did perform miracles and
did shed His blood for the sins of the world. He was raised bodily
from the grave and ascended into heaven and is coming again.
That is what the Bible says, and the Bible contains the only
documents of an historical nature concerning Him. The Bible
claims all these great cardinal facts of the faith. Evidently the
liberal is talking about another Christ, another Jesus. And any
other Christ, friends, is antichrist. Listen to the Apostle John:
"Little children, it is the last time: and as ye have heard that antichrist shall come, even now are there many antichrists;
whereby we know that it is the last time (I John 2:18).

There are a lot of antichrists. I have called your attention to
the one of liberalism but there are a lot of phonies around today
claiming to be Christ. I understand that a founder of a religion
here in Southern California is claiming today that he can do
what Christ could not do. One of the Beatles claimed that they
were more popular than Christ, and that they were able to do
more than He was able to do for our day. There are a lot of antichrists around. Our Lord did well to warn us about that.

**And when ye shall hear of wars and rumours of wars, be
ye not troubled: for such things must needs be; but the
end shall not be yet [Mark 13:7].**

And then wars, like false Christs, characterize the whole age.
No believer should be disturbed by wars. They are not the sign of
the end of the age. Neither antichrists nor wars indicate that we
are at the end of the age. When I say "antichrists" I am not

referring to *the* Antichrist. All of these false Christs are pointing to him, the final Antichrist.

> **For nation shall rise against nation, and kingdom against kingdom: and there shall be earthquakes in divers places, and there shall be famines and troubles: these are the beginnings of sorrows [Mark 13:8].**

Today man feels he is so civilized because he has so many gadgets, and he thinks he is making the world such a wonderful place. Then all of a sudden he discovers that he is polluting the earth and that he is going to make it uninhabitable. And before long, unless he cuts down the population explosion, he's going to starve to death. The Bible says, friends, that troubles and famines would come. It is interesting that this Book, which men have despised, is so accurate about it all. A few years ago men thought science would solve the problems of the world. Now we know it has made problems that neither science nor the world can solve.

Even Bernard Shaw had to say, "The science to which I pinned my faith has failed, and you are beholding an atheist who has lost his faith." What a tragedy! May I say to you, these are the things that characterize the end of the age.

> **But take heed to yourselves: for they shall deliver you up to councils; and in the synagogues ye shall be beaten: and ye shall be brought before rulers and kings for my sake, for a testimony against them.**

> **And the gospel must first be published among all nations [Mark 13:9,10].**

Now I don't think He's talking about the church here. By "gospel" He means the Gospel of the Kingdom. This is also the Gospel of grace. There are not two Gospels. The Gospel of the Kingdom is actually a facet of the Gospel of grace. All salvation is by the grace of God, and God has never had but one way to save sinners and that is by the blood of Jesus Christ. But the Gospel of the Kingdom will emphasize "Repent for the kingdom of heaven is at hand." In other words, "He is coming." And when they say it in that day, it will be in the Great Tribulation period, and it will be accurate.

But when they shall lead you, and deliver you up, take no thought beforehand what ye shall speak, neither do ye premeditate: but whatsoever shall be given you in that hour, that speak ye: for it is not ye that speak, but the Holy Ghost [Mark 13:11].

This is no verse for a lazy preacher to use as an excuse for not preparing a sermon. I remember a friend of mine down in Texas told me that he was in Temple, Texas, one morning. He had changed trains there as he was going out to a little town to preach. Another preacher there was watching him and saw him walking up and down and going over his notes for his sermon. "Are you a preacher?" my friend was asked.

"Yes,"

"What are you doing?"

"I'm going over my notes for my sermon."

"You mean that you prepare your sermon beforehand?"

"Of course, don't you?"

"No, I don't. I wait until I get up there and the Spirit of God gives me a message."

"Well, suppose the Spirit of God doesn't give you the message immediately. What do you do then?"

"Oh, I just mess around until He does."

Friends, I'm afraid there is a lot of messing around today. This verse is not talking about anything like that. This refers to the day when the 144,000 of the nation Israel are witnesses. This is a message for them in that day. This is not an excuse for you and me not to prepare our Sunday School lesson.

Now the brother shall betray the brother to death, and the father the son; and children shall rise up against their parents, and shall cause them to be put to death [Mark 13:12].

There shall be base betrayal.

And ye shall be hated of all men for my name's sake: but

he that shall endure unto the end, the same shall be saved [Mark 13:13].

There will be world-wide anti-Semitism in that day. But when God puts His seal upon them in that day, they are going to make it through to the end.

And now we come to a very dramatic part.

But when ye shall see the abomination of desolation, spoken of by Daniel the prophet, standing where it ought not, (let him that readeth understand,) then let them that be in Judaea flee to the mountains [Mark 13:14].

This is the beginning of the Great Tribulation. The first 3½ years of it are comparatively quiet; it is the false peace of the Antichrist. Then, in the midst of it, there appears this "abomination of desolation" spoken of by Daniel the prophet. It will stand where it ought not, that is, in the Holy Place. You see that if Mark had said to the Romans that the abomination of desolation would stand in the Holy Place, they would say, "Where is that?" He says it will stand where it shouldn't stand. That's more understandable to many of us too. You see, we need to understand that the Holy Place was given only to the nation Israel. It was a specific place in the Temple on earth. The church has no Holy Place.

And let him that is on the housetop not go down into the house, neither enter therein, to take any thing out of his house:

And let him that is in the field not turn back again for to take up his garment [Mark 13:15,16].

Note the urgency. They are not to go back and get their belongings but to start running.

But woe to them that are with child, and to them that give suck in those days!

And pray ye that your flight be not in the winter [Mark 13:17,18].

This is the beginning of the Great Tribulation.

> For in those days shall be affliction, such as was not
> from the beginning of the creation which God created
> unto this time, neither shall be.
>
> And except that the Lord had shortened those days, no
> flesh should be saved: but for the elect's sake, whom he
> hath chosen, he hath shortened the days.
>
> And then if any man shall say to you, Lo, here is Christ;
> or, lo, he is there; believe him not:

These will be terrible days.

> For false Christs and false prophets shall rise, and shall
> shew signs and wonders, to seduce, if it were possible,
> even the elect.
>
> But take ye heed: behold, I have foretold you all things
> [Mark 13:22,23].

False Christs and false prophets will perform genuine wonders
by the power of Satan.

The Second Coming of Christ is introduced by the darkening
of the universe, and a universal display of heavenly fireworks, a
fulfillment of Joel 2:28-32.

> But in those days, after that tribulation, the sun shall be
> darkened, and the moon shall not give her light.
>
> And the stars of heaven shall fall, and the powers that
> are in heaven shall be shaken.
>
> And then shall they see the Son of man coming in the
> clouds with great power and glory [Mark 13:24-26].

Those are not rain clouds that He is describing. They are the
glory clouds, the Shekina glory. I believe that is the sign of the
Son of man in heaven.

> And then shall he send his angels, and shall gather
> together his elect from the four winds, from the utter-
> most part of the earth to the uttermost part of heaven
> [Mark 13:27].

This is not the Rapture of the church. He doesn't send angels to gather them; rather they are caught up to meet the Lord in the air (I Thessalonians 4:13-18).

Now we come to His parable of the fig tree.

> **Now learn a parable of the fig tree: When her branch is yet tender, and putteth forth leaves, ye know that summer is near:**
>
> **So ye in like manner, when ye shall see these things come to pass, know that it is nigh, even at the doors [Mark 13:28,29].**

The fig tree speaks of the nation Israel. I recognize that there is disagreement here, and I don't mind folk disagreeing with me and thinking the fig tree means something else. But I personally believe there is Scripture to make it clear. After all, the nation Israel is God's time piece. He says we are to look to the fig tree. God's time piece is not G-R-U-E-N, nor is it B-U-L-O-V-A; God's time piece is I-S-R-A-E-L.

> **Verily I say unto you, that this generation shall not pass, till all these things be done [Mark 13:30].**

"This generation" could refer to the race of Israel. It would then teach the indestructibility of this people. Or "this generation" could refer to a generation of people and their total life span. In that case it would mean that those who saw the beginning of these events would see the conclusion of them also. The latter is the more likely meaning, it seems to me.

The emphasis appears to be on the rapidity in which these events transpire rather than upon the permanence of the nation Israel. However, both facts are sustained by Scripture.

> **Heaven and earth shall pass away: but my words shall not pass away.**
>
> **But of that day and that hour knoweth no man, no, not the angels which are in heaven, neither the Son, but the Father [Mark 13:31,32].**

This verse is admittedly difficult. If Jesus is God, it is difficult to account for this lack of omniscience. "Neither the Son" is added by Mark (compare Matthew 24:36). Mark presents Jesus as "the servant, and the servant knoweth not what his Lord doeth." The servant character of Jesus represents His most typical and true humanity. He "took upon him the form of a servant." When He became a man, He limited Himself in order to be made like us. He was not omnipresent when He became man. Martha rebuked Jesus, "Lord, if thou hadst been here, my brother had not died." It is reasonable to assume that there was a self limitation relative to His omniscience.

Take ye heed, watch and pray: for ye know not when the time is [Mark 13:33].

The proper attitude of God's people in all ages as they face the prophetic future is one of watching and praying.

For the Son of man is as a man taking a far journey, who left his house, and gave authority to his servants, and to every man his work, and commanded the porter to watch.

Watch ye therefore: for ye know not when the master of the house cometh, at even, or at midnight, or at the cockcrowing, or in the morning:

Lest coming suddenly he find you sleeping.

And what I say unto you I say unto all, Watch [Mark 13:34-37].

This parable concludes Mark's account of the Olivet Discourse. Jesus applied this parable to Himself in relationship to His Second Coming. There is a responsibility of God's people in view of the fact that Jesus will demand a report at His return. Added to praying and watching is the task of working.

This instruction is for you and me today also, although the watching is different. One can watch in anxiety and one can watch in fear. But the child of God is to be watching, looking for that blessed hope and the glorious appearing. That is joyful anticipation.

CHAPTER 14

Now, friends, we come to the longest chapter in the Gospel of Mark which has seventy-two verses. We are certainly in a chapter of action now. However, Jesus is no longer the One performing the action. He is being acted upon by others — both friends and enemies. The time has come for Him to be delivered up. His earthly ministry is concluded in the fulfillment of prophecy. "He is brought as a lamb to the slaughter" (Isaiah 53:7). He is delivering Himself into the hands of men. Mary anoints Him, Judas betrays Him, Peter denies Him, and the Sanhedrin arrests Him. He delivers Himself into the will of the Father.

As we come into the shadow of the cross, the reverent heart realizes we are on holy ground. There are depths that have not been plumbed and heights that have not been scaled. The action of this moment involves the anguish and agony of His soul. His hour has come! Do you remember that at the wedding of Cana He had said to His mother, "Mine hour is not yet come" (John 2:4)? But now it has come!

In this chapter and the one that follows there is a strange agreement of heaven and hell. Light and darkness are going together in the same direction. Righteousness and sin are going to the cross and God and Satan have decided that Jesus shall be crucified. And there are individual decisions converging upon the cross — as there are even to this day.

Here is my outline of the chapter:

1. Chief Priest and scribes plot to kill Jesus (vv. 1-2).

2. Mary of Bethany pours ointment upon the head of Jesus (vv. 3-9).

3. Judas plans to betray Jesus (vv. 10-11).

4. Jesus prepares for last Passover and first Lord's Supper (vv. 12-25).

5. Peter pledges his allegiance (vv. 26-31).

6. Jesus prays in Garden of Gethsemane (vv. 32-42).

7. Jesus placed under arrest (vv. 43-52).

8. Jesus put on trial before the Sanhedrin (vv.53-65).

9. Peter protests that he does not know Jesus (vv. 66-72).

**After two days was the feast of the passover, and of un-
leavened bread: and the chief priests and the scribes
sought how they might take him by craft, and put him to
death.**

**But they said, Not on the feast day, lest there be an up-
roar of the people [Mark 14:1,2].**

The Passover was observed on the fourteenth day of the first
month which is the Jewish month Nisan and corresponds to our
April. "In the fourteenth day of the first month at even is the
Lord's passover" (Leviticus 23:5). Then the Feast of Unleavened
Bread was on the fifteenth day of the same month and it con-
tinued for seven days thereafter. "And on the fifteenth day of the
same month is the feast of unleavened bread unto the Lord:
seven days ye must eat unleavened bread" (Leviticus 23:6). It
was, I think, the intention of these eleven rulers to take Jesus at
the end of the Passover season, after the crowds had left
Jerusalem, and then put Him to death.

They decided they would not do it on the feast day; that is,
during the Passover season, which is the Feast of Unleavened
Bread and which extends for seven days. You see, at the end of
that seven days the people would begin to leave Jerusalem and
then they would reach out and put their hands upon Him. The
reason they didn't want to touch Him during the feast days was
that they feared an uproar or a riot. The crowds were in
Jerusalem for the feast and the people held Jesus in high esteem.
The common people heard Him gladly. He fed and healed them.

**And being in Bethany in the house of Simon the leper, as
he sat at meat, there came a woman having an alabaster
box of ointment of spikenard very precious; and she
brake the box, and poured it on his head [Mark 14:3].**

Here is a lovely thing. John's Gospel places this incident six days before the Passover (John 12:1). Then have Matthew and Mark erred in placing this incident just before the Passover? No, we must remember that neither Matthew or Mark are attempting to give a chronological order. Their obvious purpose is to place this lovely incident next to the dark deed of Judas — that is, the plot to betray Jesus. They are portraying a vivid contrast and conflict of light and darkness and that is the reason they are brought together like this. Matthew and Mark do not attempt to give a chronological biography of Christ. Both friend and foe are moving toward the cross, but by different routes. Mary of Bethany is coming the way of light and love. Judas is moved by foul and dark motives. And, by the way, it is John who tells us that this woman was Mary, the sister of Martha and Lazarus (John 12:3).

> And there were some that had indignation within themselves, and said, Why was this waste of the ointment made?
>
> For it might have been sold for more than three hundred pence, and have been given to the poor. And they murmured against her [Mark 14:4,5].

John also tells us in his account that it was Judas who led in the defection, and it caused the others to follow along. The pious suggestion that the proceeds be used for charitable purposes has covered up the real reason. Judas wanted to appropriate it for his own selfish ends. Sad to say, sometimes we find the same sort of thing today in Christian work. If they had given the money to Judas, where to you think it would have gone?

> And Jesus said, Let her alone; why trouble ye her? she hath wrought a good work on me.
>
> For ye have the poor with you always, and whensoever ye will ye may do them good: but me ye have not always [Mark 14:6,7].

If they were sincere, there would be many opportunities to help the poor, and they could avail themselves of those opportunities. The presence of the poor is one of the characteristics of this age. There will be no elimination of poverty until Jesus comes. This idea today that you can eliminate poverty by handing out dollars is a big mistake. There are so many other things that are wrong in the world that must be corrected first.

> **She hath done what she could: she is come aforehand to anoint my body to the burying.**
>
> **Verily I say unto you, Wheresoever this gospel shall be preached throughout the whole world, this also that she hath done shall be spoken of for a memorial of her [Mark 14:8,9].**

She had done what she could. That is all that God has ever asked of any man to do. But the important thing to notice here is that Mary had a spiritual discernment which was sadly lacking even in the apostles at this particular time. She anointed His body for the burial. Just think of it. This poor, frail woman stood on the fringe of the events which were leading to the cross, and she let the Lord Jesus know that she understood. None of the apostles sensed this, but she did. The fragrance of the box of ointment she broke that day has been borne across the centuries by the Holy Spirit unto our day. It still fills hearts with its sweetness even at the present hour. Here in the shadow of His sufferings there was one who understood.

It is so easy to read this and it may become meaningless to us. Have any of us broken our alabaster box upon Jesus so that there might be a fragrance in our lives and it might be a blessing to others? I think that maybe if some broke their alabaster box of ointment it would be to help the poor. I'm wondering today if those who are God's people are really doing what they could do.

Now notice that right next to this lovely thing she did, the light of it and the love of it, we have the plan of Judas to betray our Lord.

> **And Judas Iscariot, one of the twelve, went unto the chief priests, to betray him unto them.**
>
> **And when they heard it, they were glad, and promised to give him money. And he sought how he might conveniently betray him [Mark 14:10,11].**

Here we see Judas in his act of darkness. This man is now plotting to put Jesus to death. The plot was to wait for a convenient time to betray Him. But, you see, the Lord upset the apple cart. We find in the Gospel of John that the Lord said to Judas, "That thou doest, do quickly" (John 13:27). So Judas must have rushed out to the Pharisees and said, "You'd better go get Him now because our plot has been discovered. He told me to do quickly that which I planned to do. He may leave town." So they got the soldiers immediately and they went out to arrest Him.

Going back to the Gospel of Mark, we find the next thing mentioned is our Lord preparing for the Passover.

> **And the first day of unleavened bread, when they killed the passover, his disciples said unto him, Where wilt thou that we go and prepare that thou mayest eat the passover? [Mark 14:12].**

The Passover was to be eaten with unleavened bread and then there were seven days of unleavened bread to follow (Exodus 12:14-20). I was in Israel at the time of the Passover, and I stayed in a hotel in Haifa. We had unleavened bread for the next seven days, and I want to tell you, friends, I got pretty tired of that bread. The rest of the food was delicious but that bread got very monotonous.

Now the disciples here were meticulous in following the letter of the Mosaic Law. They wanted to know where they were going to eat the Passover. They were going to do it right. In a few hours Jesus was to fulfill the meaning of the Passover.

> **And he sendeth forth two of his disciples, and saith unto them, Go ye into the city, and there shall meet you a man bearing a pitcher of water: follow him.**

> **And wheresoever he shall go in, say ye to the goodman of the house, The Master saith, Where is the guest-chamber, where I shall eat the passover with my disciples? [Mark 14:13, 14].**

Now again, I think this reveals the human side of our Lord, and it also reveals the fact that there were those who loved Him at this time and were preparing the Passover for Him. It also reveals the fact that our Lord was the omniscient God. Apparently the "goodman of the house" was some unnamed follower of the Lord. There is no reason to doubt that there had been a previous offer of the guest room to Jesus. I'm of the opinion that sometime during those three years of His public ministry this man had come to the Lord Jesus and he had offered this room. I think he told Jesus, "Now when You come up to Jerusalem to the Passover, I have this room for You and it will be prepared just for You." I tell you, this was a wonderful service which he performed. There are many things which we can do for the Lord Jesus, and this is what this man did.

And he will shew you a large upper room furnished and prepared: there make ready for us.

And his disciples went forth, and came into the city, and found as he had said unto them: and they made ready the passover [Mark 14:15,16].

Notice that Jesus celebrated the Passover in a borrowed room. Obviously the room had been made ready for Jesus; so I think there had been a previous commitment on this. I don't think that the host of this occasion should be blamed for not being there to wash the feet of the disciples, either. It was to be a private Passover. The Lord had said, "I shall eat the passover with my disciples" (Mark 14:14). It would be private, and the host would not interfere.

You will recall that we noted a former experience like this when Jesus sent the disciples for a donkey for Him to ride into Jerusalem. They found it as He said they would. I think there had been a previous arrangement made for the little donkey. I think our Lord was making arrangements as He went along.

And in the evening he cometh with the twelve [Mark 14:17].

Notice that He came in the evening. The Passover begins at sundown, and I think He came in under cover of darkness. He was not going to force their hand until He is ready, but at the proper time He will deliver Himself into their hands and they will crucify Him. It will not be according to their schedule but according to His schedule, by the way. This is a marvelous thing.

This was a lovely occasion. He ate the Passover with them in a leisurely and informal way. We've made our observance of the Lord's

Supper on Sunday morning a very formal service. You'll find that He ate the Passover supper here with them, and the next meal that He had with them was breakfast on the shores of the Sea of Galilee after His resurrection. I think this time was a wonderful time of fellowship.

I personally do not criticize church dinners in and of themselves. I think they can serve a wonderful purpose, but the type of church dinners we have today are often not quite what they should be. It is wonderful for people to meet and have fellowship around the person of Christ. If He is not the center, and we're just having a gay old time, though we call it fellowship, we have missed the point. A church dinner should be an occasion to meet around the person of Christ. That was the purpose of this Passover feast, by the way.

And as they sat and did eat, Jesus said, Verily I say unto you, One of you which eateth with me shall betray me.

And they began to be sorrowful, and to say unto him one by one, Is it I? and another said, Is it I? [Mark 14:18,19].

All of them knew they were capable of doing it, friends. If you have not discovered that you are totally depraved, that you are not a good person but a sinner, that you are thoroughly capable of turning your back on God, you haven't discovered very much.

Unfortunately there are people in the church who don't recognize that they are sinners and are lost. And there are saved people in the church who don't realize they are capable of turning their back on God. All of us could ask, "Is it I?"

And he answered and said unto them, It is one of the twelve, that dippeth with me in the dish.

The Son of man indeed goeth, as it is written of him: but woe to that man by whom the Son of man is betrayed! good were it for that man if he had never been born [Mark 14:20,21].

It was Judas Iscariot who had made the decision to betray Him. The responsibility of Judas was great for he had the opportunity of being with Jesus for three years. The Psalmist had written: "Yea, mine own familiar friend, in whom I trusted,

which did eat of my bread, hath lifted up his heel against me"
(Psalm 41:9). He pointed out Judas Iscariot, and I think that
Judas Iscariot left at this particular juncture.

Jesus instituted a new feast on the dying embers of the old, the
Passover feast. He reared a new monument, not a monument of
brass or marble but one that takes these elements that perish so
easily, bread and wine. The Passover had looked forward to His
coming as the Passover Lamb, and now the Lord's Supper looks
back to His death. The bread speaks of His *body* that was
broken. (Remember that not a *bone* in His body was broken.)

> **And as they did eat, Jesus took bread, and blessed, and
> brake it, and gave to them, and said, Take, eat: this is my
> body.**
>
> **And he took the cup, and when he had given thanks, he
> gave it to them: and they all drank of it.**
>
> **And he said unto them, This is my blood of the new
> testament, which is shed for many.**
>
> **Verily I say unto you, I will drink no more of the fruit of
> the vine, until that day that I drink it new in the kingdom
> of God [Mark 14:22-25].**

There are several things here that I think are interesting and
important. The Passover cup went around many times during
the Passover feast. During that time they would sing one of the
great Hallel Psalms. Apparently it was the seventh time around
when He did not drink but instituted the Lord's Supper with
them. The Lord's Supper now looks back to what He did for us
on the cross more than 1900 years ago.

The Passover looked forward to His coming, but the Passover
will be restored for the Millennial Kingdom (as we learn in
Ezekiel). And the reason for it, I think, is that during the Millennium there will be a remembrance of His coming; when it was
first instituted, it had looked forward to His coming. I see no
reason why it couldn't look forward and also look backward.
And, by the way, that would bring out the real meaning of the
Passover during the Millennial Kingdom. Paul says, "For even
Christ our passover is sacrificed for us" (I Corinthians 5:7).

And when they had sung an hymn, they went out into the mount of Olives.

And Jesus saith unto them, All ye shall be offended because of me this night: for it is written, I will smite the shepherd, and the sheep shall be scattered.

But after that I am risen, I will go before you into Galilee. But Peter said unto him, Although all shall be offended, yet will not I.

And Jesus saith unto him, Verily I say unto thee, That this day, even in this night, before the cock crow twice, thou shalt deny me thrice.

But he spake the more vehemently, If I should die with thee, I will not deny thee in any wise. Likewise also said they all [Mark 14:26-31].

We find here first that Simon Peter pledges his allegiance. He was sincere, of course, but he did not know his own weakness. That is the problem with most of us today. We don't know our own weakness. And I personally believe that you don't find out about this in psychology. I think the only place that you can really see yourself is in the Word of God. That is the only mirror that you have.

Let me quote a little excerpt of material that is being printed by a Christian organization which, I think, gives the wrong impression. It talks about a girl with a problem who went to her pastor. "After several talks together the pastor realized he was not equipped to help her as much as she could be helped. He referred Betty to a competent, Christian psychologist; one who as a professional counselor led Betty into a deeper understanding of the sources of her anxiety, many of them stemming from childhood experiences long since forgotten but recalled and understood under the guidance of a skilled helper. The result: a Christian teen released from the grip of emotional problems and given a new relationship with herself, others, and the Lord." May I say, that type of thing reads like Grimm's fairy stories — "They lived happily ever after."

Now, I happen to know that the Christian psychologist is no more competent to solve these problems today than the average pastor. I think we've been deluded today into believing that the Christian psychologist is able to say, "Hocus-pocus, abra kadabra," and somehow or another the problems are solved.

My friend, may I say to you, none of us know the depths of the human heart. Only the Word of God can let us see what sinners we are. That was the problem with Betty in the article, that is the problem with me, and that is the problem with you. When we recognize that, we see that anyone who truly knows the Word of God is able to help us. If we take the emphasis away from the Word of God, we can find that people get one problem solved with the help of the psychologist and come away with two more problems. Then the last estate of the man is worse than the first. Let's be very clear. The only solution to a problem is the Lord. You don't solve the problem so that you are enabled to go to the Lord. No, you go to the Lord and *He* is the chief and the great Physician. By the way, He is the great Psychologist and He alone knows us. In the final analysis, He is the *only* One. I am insistent in saying this, as you can see, because I think it is important today for somebody to say it. We are finding that a great many today are making merchandise of the ills of folk when actually only the Word of God can solve their ills. God Himself must do it. If we'd only learn to go to Him and cast ourselves upon Him. Maybe we recognize that we have had a bad childhood — friends, we've had a bad everything! But we have a Saviour who loves us, and we can go to Him. How wonderful it is to have Someone to go to.

We find the Lord Jesus now telling them that He is going before into Galilee. He announces His resurrection. He tells them the sheep are going to be scattered but He will go on into Galilee after His resurrection. He promised to meet them there. But Simon Peter couldn't let it go at that. He declares that he will not be offended even if the others are. Here again we see that he just doesn't know what he is saying. So our Lord prepares him for what is coming. And He lets Peter know that He is going to stand by him.

My friend, the Lord will stand by you in times like this. He will be there in our most desperate and dastardly hour. He certainly was with this man Peter.

And they came to a place which was named Gethsemane: and he saith to his disciples, Sit ye here, while I shall pray.

And he taketh with him Peter and James and John, and began to be sore amazed, and to be very heavy;

And saith unto them, My soul is exceeding sorrowful unto death: tarry ye here, and watch [Mark 14:32-34].

The Garden of Gethsemane must have been a familiar spot to which they came rather frequently. Whether it is the "Garden of Gethsemane" as it is known today we do not know. I am of the opinion that it should be on the other side of the mountain — but the location is really immaterial. Since they came here rather frequently, it was a place that Judas knew. Our Lord never spent a night inside the city of Jerusalem. He went out to this place.

There are only eleven disciples now. He leaves an outer circle of eight. He takes three of them, Peter, James, and John, a step closer to Him in this hour. He went to pray. The language indicates that He faced a sore ordeal in the garden. "Began to be sore *amazed*" is actually *startled* or more intense — we would say *stunned*. It says that He was very "heavy" which literally is *distressed*.

He faces here a travail of soul that was as great, if not greater, than the suffering of the body on the cross. Did He face the tempter again here in the garden? I think He did. I must be very frank and say that we can only stand here on the fringe. There are mysteries in the garden that we cannot understand. I think it is audacious and actually borders on the blasphemous for people to sing, "I'll go with Him through the garden." I'm sorry, friend, if you don't mind, I'll beg off. I can't go with Him through the garden. You don't know how weak and stumbling and bumbling I really am. I can't go with Him through the garden but I will stand at the edge and watch Him pray. He asked us to watch and pray so that we enter not into temptation.

And he went forward a little, and fell on the ground, and prayed that, if it were possible, the hour might pass from him.

And he said, Abba, Father, all things are possible unto

**thee; take away this cup from me: nevertheless not what I
will, but what thou wilt [Mark 14:35,36].**

Mark says that He prayed that the hour might pass from Him.
It was not *death* He dreaded but rather the *hour* of the cross —
that moment when sin was to be put upon Him. He was made sin
for us (II Corinthians 5:21). Mark makes the "hour" and the
"cup" synonymous.

Listen to the writer to the Hebrews: "Who in the days of his
flesh, when he had offered up prayers and supplications with
strong crying and tears unto him that was able to save him from
death, and was heard in that he feared; though he were a Son,
yet learned he obedience by the things which he suffered"
(Hebrews 5:7,8).

Now He returns to the place He had stationed the three disciples.

**And he cometh, and findeth them sleeping, and saith
unto Peter, Simon, sleepest thou? couldest not thou
watch one hour?**

**Watch ye and pray, lest ye enter into temptation. The
spirit truly is ready, but the flesh is weak [Mark 14:37,38].**

The three disciples were not at all alarmed. In fact, they could
sleep through it all. This man, Peter, wasn't even disturbed that
he was going to deny Christ. He should have been watching and
praying, but he just went off to sleep. Watching and praying is
the way for us to avoid temptation today, friends.

Now you'll notice that Jesus goes back and He repeats the first
prayer.

**And again he went away, and prayed, and spake the
same words [Mark 14:39].**

And the disciples went to sleep again.

**And when he returned, he found them asleep again, (for
their eyes were heavy,) neither wist they what to answer
him [Mark 14:40].**

They had no explanation for their failure. We certainly learn here that the flesh cannot be trusted.

And he cometh the third time, and saith unto them, Sleep on now, and take your rest: it is enough, the hour is come; behold, the Son of man is betrayed into the hands of sinners.

Rise up, let us go; lo, he that betrayeth me is at hand [Mark 14:41,42].

Apparently there was a lapse of time in here so that they had a brief sleep before He was arrested.

And immediately, while he yet spake, cometh Judas, one of the twelve, and with him a great multitude with swords and staves, from the chief priests and the scribes and the elders [Mark 14:43].

Now you see that they have come out to do the thing that they said they would not do. They had said, "Not during the feast days."

And he that betrayed him had given them a token, saying, Whomsoever I shall kiss, that same is he; take him, and lead him away safely [Mark 14:44].

Here we have recorded one of the basest acts of treachery. It is foul and loathsome. Judas knew our Lord's accustomed place of retirement and he led the enemy there.

A kiss is a badge of love and affection and Judas used it to betray Christ. This makes his act even more dastardly and repugnant. Incidentally, we learn here that our Lord in His humanity looked no different from other men. He needed to be identified in a crowd.

And as soon as he was come, he goeth straightway to him, and saith, Master, master; and kissed him [Mark 14:45].

You will notice that Judas calls Him, "Master." He does not call Him "Lord." "No man can say that Jesus is the Lord, but by the Holy Ghost" (I Corinthians 12:3).

And they laid their hands on him, and took him [Mark 14:46].

This marks the moment that Jesus was delivered into the hands of sinful men. He yields Himself now to go to the cross.

Simon Peter attempts to come to His rescue:

And one of them that stood by drew a sword, and smote a servant of the high priest, and cut off his ear.

And Jesus answered and said unto them, Are ye come out, as against a thief, with swords and with staves to take me?

I was daily with you in the temple teaching, and ye took me not: but the scriptures must be fulfilled [Mark 14:47-49].

Jesus points out that this fulfills prophecy. If these people had believed their own Scriptures, they might have hesitated or even changed their minds.

And they all forsook him, and fled [Mark 14:50].

As we suspected, it was Peter who cut off the man's ear with his sword. John also tells us that the man's name was Malchus. Simon Peter was a pretty good fisherman but a pretty sorry swordsman. He had intended to get the neck but he missed it and got an ear.

"They all forsook Him and fled" is a fulfillment of prophecy.

Then we have here this incident of a certain young man.

And there followed him a certain young man, having a linen cloth cast about his naked body; and the young men laid hold on him:

And he left the linen cloth, and fled from them naked [Mark 14:51,52].

There has always been speculation as to who this is. Some think it may have been the apostle Paul. Some think it may have been John Mark. I personally think it would be more apt to be John Mark.

And they led Jesus away to the high priest: and with him were assembled all the chief priests and the elders and the scribes [Mark 14:53].

Jesus is now brought before Caiaphas, the high priest who was acceptable to Rome. Annas, his father-in-law, was actually the high priest according to the Mosaic Law. Jesus was first brought before Annas, which John records. Some believe that Annas was the real rascal behind the plot to kill Jesus. This is a meeting of the Sanhedrin.

And Peter followed him afar off, even into the palace of the high priest: and he sat with the servants, and warmed himself at the fire [Mark 14:54].

Peter is moving toward his shameful fall. He followed afar off and then sits with the wrong crowd.

And the chief priests and all the council sought for witness against Jesus to put him to death; and found none [Mark 14:55].

The meeting of the Sanhedrin was illegal since it was at night. Their method was likewise illegal. They heard only witnesses who were against Jesus.

For many bare false witness against him, but their witness agreed not together.

And there arose certain, and bare false witness against him, saying,

We heard him say, I will destroy this temple that is made with hands, and within three days I will build another made without hands.

But neither so did their witness agree together [Mark 14:56-59].

Many were willing to bear false witness, but no two agreed. A charge had to be established in the mouth of at least two witnesses. Of course Jesus did not say that He would destroy the temple and then raise it up in three days. He said, "Destroy this temple" that is, *you* destroy this temple; and John explains, "But he spoke of the temple of his body" (John 2:21).

And the high priest stood up in the midst, and asked Jesus, saying, Answerest thou nothing? what is it which these witness against thee?

But he held his peace, and answered nothing. Again the high priest asked him, and said unto him, Art thou the Christ, the Son of the Blessed?

And Jesus said, I am: and ye shall see the Son of man sitting on the right hand of power, and coming in the clouds of heaven [Mark 14:60-62].

Jesus did not defend Himself against such obvious falsehood. Again He was fulfilling prophecy: ". . . as a sheep before her shearers is dumb, so he openeth not his mouth" (Isaiah 53:7). The silence of Jesus surprised and annoyed the high priest. He wanted Jesus to answer to see if He might condemn Himself. Finally the high priest put Him under oath. Under oath Jesus claimed to be the Messiah, the Son of God. He could make no higher claim. He added a claim that could only pertain to the Son of God: "I saw in the night visions, and, behold, one like the Son of man came with the clouds of heaven, and came to the Ancient of days, and they brought him near before him. And there was given him dominion, and glory, and a kingdom, that all people, nations, and languages, should serve him: his dominion is an everlasting dominion, which shall not pass away, and his kingdom that which shall not be destroyed" (Daniel 7:13,14].

The high priest understood what he said and all the implications of it. He displayed his intense emotion by tearing his garment. In doing this, he broke the Mosaic Law, as the garment of the high priest was not to be torn.

Then the high priest rent his clothes, and saith, What need we any further witnesses?

Ye have heard the blasphemy: what think ye? And they all condemned him to be guilty of death.

And some began to spit on him, and to cover his face, and to buffet him, and to say unto him, Prophesy: and the servants did strike him with the palms of their hands [Mark 14:63-65].

They condemned Him to die because He claimed to be the Messiah. The charge was changed when they went before Pilate (Mark 15:3). Their treatment of Him was the worst indignity He could endure. Imagine spitting in the face of the Son of God!

While the farce of the trial of Jesus was in progress, Simon Peter was in the place of great temptation.

> **And as Peter was beneath in the palace, there cometh one of the maids of the high priest:**
>
> **And when she saw Peter warming himself, she looked upon him, and said, And thou also wast with Jesus of Nazareth.**
>
> **But he denied, saying, I know not, neither understand I what thou sayest. And he went out into the porch; and the cock crew.**
>
> **And a maid saw him again, and began to say to them that stood by, This is one of them.**
>
> **And he denied it again. And a little after, they that stood by said again to Peter, Surely thou art one of them: for thou art a Galilaean, and thy speech agreeth thereto [Mark 14:66-70].**

A little wisp of a maid caused him to deny His Lord. Peter was ashamed to be known as a follower of Jesus at this time. Have we ever been in a similar position? May God forgive our cowardice and weakness as He did that of Peter.

On the third encounter notice that Peter's weakness in wanting to talk too much got him into trouble. His speech gave him away.

> **But he began to curse and to swear, saying, I know not this man of whom ye speak.**
>
> **And the second time the cock crew. And Peter called to mind the word that Jesus said unto him, Before the cock crow twice, thou shalt deny me thrice. And when he thought thereon, he wept [Mark 14:71,72].**

This man had not known his own weakness. Simon Peter loved

Jesus and he was sincere when he promised to be loyal to Him. But he did not know himself. He had not yet come to the place where he saw no good in the flesh at all.

However, Peter could repent of his sin, and that is the real test of a genuine believer. These were tears of heartbroken repentance. Years later in his epistle he wrote, "Who are kept by the power of God through faith unto salvation ready to be revealed in the last time" (I Peter 1:5). Peter knew that the Lord Jesus had kept him!

We close this chapter with Jesus in the hands of His enemies. His own are scattered. One has betrayed Him; another has denied Him. It is the night of sin!

CHAPTER 15

We are now in the study of the crucifixion of Christ. I know that all Scripture is given by inspiration of God and it is profitable (II Tomothy 3:16), but this portion that describes the death and resurrection of Christ has particular meaning for us today. We closed the last chapter with Jesus in the hands of His enemies. His own are scattered. One has betrayed Him. Another has denied Him.

Sin is the issue this night in two different ways. Sin is trying to destroy Him. And He is doing something about sin — He is dying for your sin and my sin. I suppose it can be said that the cross is one of the many paradoxes of the Christian faith for that reason. It is at once the greatest tragedy of the ages, and the most glorious victory of earth and heaven. Therefore, we should not come to this chapter with a feeling of defeat or sympathy for the Sufferer. We should walk softly and reverently through these scenes, with a heart welling up to God in thanksgiving for providing so great salvation.

The tragic note is inescapable in these scenes with the cruel injustice and bitter suffering inflicted upon Jesus. It is no wonder that Clovis, the barbarian, when he first heard the Gospel read, exclaimed, "If I had only been there with my soldiers." But remember, it is not our sympathy that the Son of God wants. He wants our *faith*. Believe on the Lord Jesus Christ. "That if thou shalt confess with thy mouth the Lord Jesus, and shalt believe in thine heart that God hath raised him from the dead, thou shalt be saved. For with the heart man believeth unto righteousness; and with the mouth confession is made unto salvation" (Romans 10:9,10). He wants the *faith* of your heart, not the *sympathy* of your heart.

Mark is the Gospel of action, and this fifteenth chapter sets forth the supreme nature of the action. The crucifixion is the climactic point and crowning event of this action. It is the crucifixion toward which all creation and the purposes of God were moving from all eternity, for He was the "Lamb slain from the foundation of the world." The Gospel is now translated into action! Paul could say later on, "For I delivered unto you first of all that which I also received, how that Christ died for our sins according to the scriptures; and that he was buried, and that he rose again the third day according to the scriptures" (I Corinthians 15:3,4).

You see, the Gospel is what *He* did. It is not what God is asking *you* to do. It is *His* action, not your action or mine. You and I are in no position to do anything that would be acceptable to God. Your righteousness and my righteousness are not acceptable for salvation. God must and does provide that righteousness in Christ. He was delivered for our offences and was raised again for our justification, for our righteousness (Romans 4:25).

Now I will give an outline for this fifteenth chapter:

1. Jesus carried before Pilate (vv. 1-6).

2. Jesus condemned — Barabbas released (vv. 7-15).

3. Jesus crowned with thorns (vv. 16-23).

4. Jesus crucified (vv. 24-41).

5. Jesus committed to Joseph — New Tomb (vv. 42-47).

And straightway in the morning the chief priests held a consultation with the elders and scribes and the whole council, and bound Jesus, and carried him away, and delivered him to Pilate [Mark 15:1].

The reason that they did this was that the Sanhedrin could condemn Jesus to die, but they could not carry out the execution. Only Rome could do that. Therefore, this body had to appeal to the Roman court for the execution of the death penalty that they had decided upon. Now the charge which they had brought against Him in the Sanhedrin would never stand up before Pilate. So they met early the next morning to formulate charges that would stand up before the Roman court and would make *legal* the illegal action of the night before.

You see, Pilate is the Roman governor who is in Jerusalem at this time. His headquarters were down at Caesarea because he liked that place — it was on the seacoast and it had a delightful climate. He didn't like Jerusalem. He came up there only at feast times to keep down any riots. The Roman government didn't permit riots and protest marches and that type of thing, which is one reason Rome stood for about one thousand years as a great world empire. I think that present-day nations need to take note of this.

Pilate was a politician. Expediency rather than Roman justice was the motivating force in his life. He actually sought to release Jesus when he discovered He was innocent, but at the same time he wanted to please the religious rulers. Yet, if you will notice here, he couldn't really get the cooperation from Jesus that he hoped to get. He thought that if Jesus would cooperate, he could please the religious rulers, too. Pilate is a typical example of a cheap politician who is unloosed from the noble moorings of honesty and integrity and 'carries water on both shoulders,' seeking to compromise and to please all sides. And when you try to do that, you please no one.

> **And Pilate asked him, Art thou the King of the Jews? And he answering said unto him, Thou sayest it [Mark 15:2].**

That would be the same as saying, "You're right. I am."

> **And the chief priests accused him of many things: but he answered nothing.**

> **And Pilate asked him again, saying, Answerest thou nothing? behold how many things they witness against thee.**

> **But Jesus yet answered nothing; so that Pilate marvelled.**

> **Now at that feast he released unto them one prisoner, whomsoever they desired [Mark 15:3-6].**

Pilate was amazed and shocked at a prisoner who would stand before him and not defend himself. I imagine that other prisoners went to great lengths to defend themselves, but this Prisoner was different. He didn't defend Himself and Pilate wanted to know the reason.

Now, when we compare the Gospel of John, we will find that

there was a great deal of interplay back and forth between Pilate
and the religious rulers as Pilate actually sought to deliver Jesus.
He took Him on the inside to talk to Him. Then he came back
out and then took Him in again, hoping to get His cooperation.
But Pilate found out that he had to stand on his own two feet and
make a decision relative to Jesus Christ. For that matter, that is
exactly what every man and every woman has to do.

Pilate then thought he could get off the hook by releasing a
prisoner. This man just couldn't believe that anyone would ask
for Barabbas to be delivered and for Jesus to be crucified. He
really thought that he had found a solution for the dilemma in
which he found himself.

> **And there was one named Barabbas, which lay bound
> with them that had made insurrection with him, who had
> committed murder in the insurrection [Mark 15:7].**

Here was a man guilty of murder and guilty of leading an insurrection. He was the chief prisoner at that time. He was actually to be crucified along with the others. I think the Lord
Jesus was crucified on the cross intended for Barabbas.

> **But Pilate answered them saying, Will ye that I release
> unto you the King of the Jews?**
>
> **For he knew that the chief priests had delivered him for
> envy.**
>
> **But the chief priests moved the people, that he should
> rather release Barabbas unto them.**
>
> **And Pilate answered and said again unto them, What
> will ye then that I shall do unto him whom ye call the
> King of the Jews?**
>
> **And they cried out again, Crucify him [Mark 15:9-13].**

A very remarkable and unheard of thing is taking place here. It
was evident to Pilate that the charges brought against Jesus were
false. Here he had on his hands a prisoner who was an outstanding criminal, and so he makes the comparison between Jesus
and Barabbas. He thought for certain that the people wouldn't
dare ask for Barabbas to be released and for Jesus to be crucified.

He just didn't know the depths to which people can sink. He didn't know the depths to which religion can sink. He was so shocked when they asked for Barabbas to be released that he, the judge, asked the people in consternation what he should do then with Jesus.

Then Pilate said unto them, Why, what evil hath he done? And they cried out the more exceedingly, Crucify him [Mark 15:14].

The mob had been instructed to demand that Jesus be crucified. Here we see mob rule with a vengeance. When Pilate asked what evil Jesus had done, they simply cried out more and more, "Crucify Him." No mob is prepared to reason or to use its head or use good judgment. All they can do is cry out, "Crucify Him."

And so Pilate, willing to content the people, released Barabbas unto them, and delivered Jesus, when he had scourged him, to be crucified [Mark 15:15].

Pilate obviously was a weak, vacillating politician. He yielded to the cry of the mob and he delivered the Lord Jesus to be crucified. Roman justice certainly went awry here. An innocent man is to die. But wait a minute — He is taking my place and I am *not* innocent. He's taking your place also.

And the soldiers led him away into the hall, called Praetorium; and they call together the whole band [Mark 15:16].

When any criminal was to be crucified, he was turned over to these soldiers. They were a brutal lot, and they could do as they pleased with the prisoner. They, of course, humiliated their prisoners, tortured them, and made them a plaything for their sadistic appetites. This is the thing they do now with the Lord Jesus.

I've suggested that they played a game, a Roman game called "hot hand." They would all stick their fist up in the face of Jesus; then they would blindfold Him and all but one would hit Him. They beat His face into a pulp until I don't think He looked like a man. Of course, when they would take the blindfold off, He had to pick out the fist that had not hit Him. The prisoner never

could pick out the right one. Even if he did, they wouldn't admit
it was the right one because they were going to play that game
again and again. It was a vicious beating, which is probably the
reason we are told that they had to get this man Simon of Cyrene
to carry the cross. Our Lord was thirty-three years old — He still
had the strength of youth. I'm confident He was muscular. He
had walked up and down that country. He'd been a carpenter,
and He'd been able to drive the money-changers out. But they
had beaten Him unmercifully.

> **And they clothed him with purple, and platted a crown
> of thorns, and put it about his head,**
>
> **And began to salute him, Hail, King of the Jews! [Mark
> 15:17,18].**

The act of putting a purple robe and crown of thorns on Him
was mere mockery.

> **And they smote him on the head with a reed, and did
> spit upon him, and bowing their knees worshipped him
> [Mark 15:19].**

This was vicious. The imperfect tense of the verbs indicates
that they kept on smiting Him and spitting on Him. This is more
than ordinary human hatred. This was brutal and cruel, reveal-
ing the degradation of the human heart. Do you see what He en-
dured when He took your place? The cross is still before Him.

> **And when they had mocked him, they took off the purple
> from him, and put his own clothes on him, and led him
> out to crucify him.**
>
> **And they compel one Simon a Cyrenian, who passed by,
> coming out of the country, the father of Alexander and
> Rufus, to bear his cross [Mark 15:20,21].**

After a morning of inhuman suffering they led Him away to be
crucified. Simon was from Cyrene in North Africa. He probably
was attending the Passover in Jerusalem. It appears that he was
picked out of the crowd by chance to help carry the cross. It is
believed that Jesus carried the cross to the city gates.

> **And they bring him unto the place Golgotha, which is,**

being interpreted, The place of a skull [Mark 15:22].

"Golgotha" means the place of a skull. Our word is *Calvary*.

And they gave him to drink wine mingled with myrrh: but he received it not [Mark 15:23].

The wine mingled with myrrh was a drug to help deaden the awful ordeal of the cross for those about to die. It is interesting to note that when He was born, wise men brought Him myrrh. When He died, He was offered myrrh. Myrrh speaks of His death.

And when they had crucified him, they parted his garments, casting lots upon them, what every man should take [Mark 15:24].

Actually, a better translation here would be "*after* they crucified him" No Gospel writer records the details of the crucifixion; they give us only incidents around the crucifixion. The Spirit of God drew a veil over it as if to say, "There is nothing here to satisfy sadistic gossip. There is nothing here with which an idle mind should be occupied. It is too horrible."

The parting of His garments was in fulfillment of the prophecy in Psalm 22:18.

And it was the third hour, and they crucified him.

And the superscription of his accusation was written over, THE KING OF THE JEWS [Mark 15:25,26].

Now we are told here that it was the third hour when they crucified Him, which was nine o'clock in the morning. (Mark uses the Hebrew computation of time, while John uses the Roman.) We must put all the Gospel writing together to get the full superscription. John tells us that it was written in Hebrew, Greek, and Latin. No Gospel writer is intending to give us the whole story.

The charge for which they crucified Him was this:

"THE KING OF THE JEWS"

It may seem an anomalous statement to say that it was true. It was not true in the way they meant it. He had led no insurrection against Rome. He offered Himself to Israel and was rejected.

And with him they crucify two thieves; the one on his right hand, and the other on his left.

And the scripture was fulfilled, which saith, And he was numbered with the transgressors [Mark 15:27,28].

Jesus was crucified, we are told, with two thieves; the one on His right hand, and the other on His left. And that was done, Mark says, so that the Scripture might be fulfilled. Then he quotes Isaiah 53:12, "And he was numbered with the transgressors."

And they that passed by railed on him, wagging their heads, and saying, Ah, thou that destroyest the temple, and buildest it in three days,

Save thyself, and come down from the cross.

Likewise also the chief priests mocking said among themselves with the scribes, He saved others; himself he cannot save [Mark 15:29-31].

This was true. He could not save others and at the same time save Himself. He gave Himself for others — this is the great principle of redemption.

Let Christ the King of Israel descend now from the cross, that we may see and believe. And they that were crucified with him reviled him.

And when the sixth hour was come, there was darkness over the whole land until the ninth hour.

And at the ninth hour Jesus cried with a loud voice, saying, Eloi, Eloi, lama sabachthani? which is, being interpreted, My God, my God, why hast thou forsaken me? [Mark 15:32-34].

I want you to notice here that Mark gives us the crucifixion by the clock. On the third hour He was put on the cross, and at the sixth hour (which would be twelve noon) darkness came down. The high noon sun was covered and darkness came down over the cross. From the sixth hour to the ninth hour, that would be until three o'clock in the afternoon, there was darkness.

Now will you notice this: the first three hours were from 9:00 A.M. until 12 noon, the second three hours were from 12 noon to 3:00 P.M. Jesus hung on the cross for six hours. In the first three hours there was physical light; in the second three hours there was physical darkness. But in the first three hours there was spiritual darkness; in the second three hours there was spiritual light. Why? Because in those first three hours man did his worst. They crucified Him and they reviled Him. Even those who were hanging with Him on the cross reviled him. At least at the first, both thieves did. Then the enemy marching around down beneath were wagging their heads and ridiculing Him. In the first three hours man is working, doing his very worst; in the second three hours God is working. He was suffering at the hands of man in the first three hours; He was suffering *for* man in the last three hours. In the first three hours He was dying because of sin; in the second three hours He was dying for the sin of the world. So in the time of the physical darkness, there was actually spiritual light and God was working. In those first three hours sin was doing all it could to destroy Him; in the second three hours He is making His soul an offering for sin. In those last three hours He is paying for the sins of the world. It was during this period that He was made sin for us; He became sin for us. He was forsaken of God and yet, even at that time, God was in Christ, reconciling the world unto Himself (II Corinthians 5:19). What a paradox we find here.

And some of them that stood by, when they heard it, said, Behold, he calleth Elias.

And one ran and filled a spunge full of vinegar, and put it on a reed, and gave him to drink, saying, Let alone; let us see whether Elias will come to take him down [Mark 15:35,36].

The crowd misunderstood what He said. They probably thought that He had called for Elijah because of the similarity of the words and they said, "Let us see whether Elijah will come." You wonder whether they didn't halfway suspect that He really was the Messiah. I think there is something in the human heart that would tell them — and did tell them — this was the Messiah.

Then they gave Him some wine to quench His thirst. This was not the drug that they gave Him later on. He took this in order to fulfill the prophecy: "They gave me also gall for my meat; and in my thirst they gave me vinegar to drink" (Psalm 69:21).

And Jesus cried with a loud voice, and gave up the ghost.

And the veil of the temple was rent in twain from the top to the bottom [Mark 15:37,38].

He did not die because the bodily organs refused to function. He surrendered up His Spirit.

The rending of the veil was evidently witnessed by many priests. At three o'clock was the time of the evening sacrifice and they were serving in the Temple at that very moment. This must have had some effect on them. At any rate, we note later on that many of the priests came to a saving knowledge of Christ. "And the word of God increased and the number of the disciples multiplied in Jerusalem greatly; and a great company of the priests were obedient to the faith" (Acts 6:7). This reveals that many of the priests believed on the Lord Jesus Christ, and we have every reason to believe that some of them were serving in the Temple at the time of the crucifixion.

The fact that the very moment when He gave up the ghost was the moment that the veil was rent in twain is not accidental by any means. They are specifically stated together.

Jesus gave up the ghost. He could not die until He had given up His Spirit. He did not die because His bodily organs refused to function, which means He died differently, of course, from any of us. I've been in the presence of quite a few people when they have died. These folk, I've always noticed, have a death rattle. The last thing we do is try to draw in our breath. The one thing we want is that final breath. He didn't do that. He dismissed His Spirit. So that certainly made His death different even in a physical sense.

At that very instant, the veil was torn in two. The veil speaks of the humanity of Christ. The book of Leviticus gives us more understanding of the veil because the book of Leviticus has to do with the service in the Tabernacle. That veil, you will recall, speaks of the humanity of Christ, and this carries a tremendous message. You see, the humanity of Christ, or the life of Christ, shuts us out from God. His sinless life shows how sinful ours is. The minute He died, the veil was rent. It is His death that brings us to God, friends, not His life.

And when the centurion, which stood over against him, saw that he so cried out, and gave up the ghost, he said, Truly this man was the Son of God [Mark 15:39].

I believe that this was the confession of faith in this centurion and this was as far as he could go at this time. He couldn't have said anything that would have revealed his faith more than this. He acknowledged that Jesus is God's Son. He acknowledged who He was and certainly what He was doing. I do not believe that this man had all the details of theology. This man had never read Strong's theology or any of my books, but this man knew enough to take his place beneath the cross of Christ. And, you know, that is all God has ever asked any sinner to do. He asks us to come in faith to Him. That is what this man is doing. We must remember that he was a pagan Roman, and he had the cruel job of crucifying men. He was certainly made very tender at this time.

Now we are told about these women who were present.

There were also women looking on afar off: among whom was Mary Magdalene, and Mary the mother of James the less and of Joses, and Salome;

(Who also, when he was in Galilee, followed him, and ministered unto him;) and many other women which came up with him unto Jerusalem [Mark 15:40,41].

It is interesting to note, by the way, that the women were the last at the cross and the first at the tomb. These stood afar off, we're told here. They remained faithful. They were the ones who were faithful to the very end. His disciples and apostles were scattered at this time. There are other women who are not named here at all for it says, "and many other women which came up with him unto Jerusalem."

And now when the even was come, because it was the preparation, that is, the day before the sabbath,

Joseph of Arimathaea, an honourable counsellor, which also waited for the kingdom of God, came, and went in boldly unto Pilate, and craved the body of Jesus.

And Pilate marvelled if he were already dead: and calling unto him the centurion, he asked him whether he had been any while dead.

And when he knew it of the centurion, he gave the body to Joseph [Mark 15:42-45].

This is something that is quite interesting to note. Joseph of Arimathaea is a little-known follower of Jesus. He actually had charge of the burial, and He had the courage to step out in the open here. He was a member of the Sanhedrin (Luke 23:51,52), and this man had not consented to the counsel and the deed of that group. He was of Arimathaea, a city of that land. He also was waiting for the Kingdom of God. This man now steps out as a follower of the Lord Jesus when the apostles were scattered, gone under cover, and he asked for the body of Jesus.

We're told here that Pilate marvelled that He was so soon dead. The reason is that customarily a person who was crucified would linger alive on a cross, sometimes for days. His life would just gradually expire. It was a cruel and inhuman mode of torture. This is the reason Pilate marvelled and made special inquiry. Jesus gave up the ghost. That is important for us to see. During the last hours of dying, a prisoner on the cross had his legs broken to hasten his death. But Jesus was already dead and it was not necessary to break His legs. That, you know, was a fulfillment of prophecy that not a bone of His body would be broken.

Pilate, we are told, gave the body to Joseph. It is interesting to note that there are two words used for "body" in this section.

Joseph asked for the body — *soma* is the Greek word.

Pilate gave him the body — *ptoma* is the Greek word.

The first speaks of the total personality, and it is a word of care and tenderness. The word used when Pilate gave the body just means the corpse or the carcass. It is a different viewpoint and attitude toward death and toward the bodies of those that are dead. The word Joseph used was a word of tenderness for the body. He wanted Jesus. All Pilate did was to give him a carcass. What a difference that is!

Friends, only the Lord Jesus can put any value on you. You and I are not worth very much, but He paid a tremendous price for our redemption. We groan within these bodies, but even our bodies are to be redeemed. There is a day coming when we will experience the redemption of our bodies. That is just a little added insight here.

Notice that Joseph is called a rich man and he put away the body tenderly into his new tomb.

And he bought fine linen, and took him down, and wrapped him in the linen, and laid him in a sepulchre which was hewn out of a rock, and rolled a stone unto the door of the sepulchre [Mark 15:46].

That door was sealed. The Romans sealed the rock and guarded it with Roman soldiers (Matthew 27:66).

And Mary Magdalene and Mary the mother of Joses beheld where he was laid [Mark 15:47].

The women were the only mourners. They were with Him to the very end. God bless the women.

CHAPTER 16

Now we come to the resurrection and ascension of Jesus. The bodily resurrection of Jesus is one of the cardinal doctrines of the Christian faith. It is the heart of the primitive Gospel. Every sermon in the book of Acts is a message on the resurrection — every speaker got to this subject. The early Church dwelt upon it constantly. Today there is scant reference to the resurrection, and in many churches there is one sermon preached each year on Easter Sunday with the message of the resurrection. "He is risen!" That is the thrilling message which electrified a lethargic and sinful generation in the Roman Empire. It turned them upside down, wrong side out, and right side up; and they went out to tell the world about it. There would be hope today if the church would preach this truth with much *assurance*.

Let me mention here that this chapter has been under severe criticism by the higher critics. I mention this so someone doesn't wonder why I do not mention the textual problem here. Verses 9-20 have been called in question by the textual scholars of both the conservative and liberal groups. Wescott and Hort omit it from their Greek text, but they do include it in smaller type. Nestle follows the same procedure by separating it from the regular text. Some, from the liberal wing, omit it altogether.

It is true that two of the better manuscripts omit it entirely. Aleph and the Vatican manuscripts end Mark's Gospel at verse 8 of chapter 16.

It is not my intention to go into a discussion in the field of New Testament Introduction. Rather, I am interested in giving attention to the meaning of the text. I believe that these last twelve verses are a part of the inspired Scripture, and shall treat them as any other portion of the Word of God. The omission of this portion from two of our better manuscripts is not sufficient grounds to remove it from Scripture, especially when all the other manuscripts and uncials contain it. The internal evidence is not enough to dismiss it either, as the style is still that of Mark — brief and blunt.

Here is my outline of the last chapter of the Gospel of Mark.

1. The arrival of the women at the empty tomb (vv. 1-4).

2. The announcement of the angel that Jesus had risen (vv. 5-8).

3. The appearances of Jesus (vv. 9-18).

4. The ascension of Jesus (vv. 19,20).

And when the sabbath was past, Mary Magdalene, and Mary the mother of James, and Salome, had bought sweet spices, that they might come and anoint him [Mark 16:1].

This was now early on Sunday morning, the first day of the week. They were never able to anoint His body. It was not Mary of Bethany who wasted her ointment, but these women wasted theirs because when they brought it to the tomb, Jesus was gone — He was alive again.

And very early in the morning the first day of the week, they came unto the sepulchre at the rising of the sun.

And they said among themselves, Who shall roll us away the stone from the door of the sepulchre?

And when they looked, they saw that the stone was rolled away: for it was very great [Mark 16:2-4].

The Sabbath had ended at sundown on Saturday. They had secured the spices sometime after that in order to make the trip to the tomb so early on Sunday morning. The same women who were present at the cross, came to the tomb. I think it is accurate to state that the women were the last at the cross and the first at the tomb.

The attitude of the disciples was that since Jesus was dead, it was better to stay under cover until after all the excitement had died down and they were no longer in danger. Did they intend to go to the tomb? There is no evidence to support such an intention. It seems that none of them intended to visit that tomb.

Now it was very early at sunrise and these women intended to anoint the body of Jesus with the spices they had bought. They were presented with the difficulty of getting into the tomb because of the stone at the door. They found that their difficulty was dissolved by the fact that the stone had been rolled away. The body of Jesus was gone. There was a heavenly messenger with the first announcement of the resurrection. The fact that the tomb was empty has been well attested and established. The evidence is such that it would be acceptable in a court of law.

> **And entering into the sepulchre, they saw a young man sitting on the right side, clothed in a long white garment; and they were affrighted.**

> **And he saith unto them, Be not affrighted: Ye seek Jesus of Nazareth, which was crucified: he is risen; he is not here: behold the place where they laid him.**

> **But go your way, tell his disciples and Peter that he goeth before you into Galilee; there shall ye see him, as he said unto you [Mark 16:5-7].**

To study the facts of the empty tomb we need to put the four Gospel records together. Some of the facts are in Matthew and others are in John's Gospel. Right here I want to quote a statement given by Lord Lyndhurst, High Chancellor of Great Britain — 1846, and High Steward of Cambridge, the highest honor which they confer. This man said, "I know pretty well what evidence is; and, I tell you, such evidence as that for the Resurrection has never broken down yet."

The women were specifically told to go and report to the disciples. (The angel surely was not waiting for some disciple to come by, as we can see from the message he sends to them. Jesus will meet them in Galilee as He had promised them. John 21 tells us of that remarkable meeting.) You can imagine the amazement of these women. They were speechless. And this, frankly, doesn't seem to me to be an appropriate place for Mark to end his Gospel as some of the critics claim.

> **And they went out quickly, and fled from the sepulchre; for they trembled and were amazed: neither said they any thing to any man; for they were afraid [Mark 16:8].**

Now we come to the section that is not included in all the manuscripts but which we believe is the Word of God.

Now when Jesus was risen early the first day of the week, he appeared first to Mary Magdalene, out of whom he had cast seven devils.

And she went and told them that had been with him, as they mourned and wept.

And they, when they had heard that he was alive, and had been seen of her, believed not.

After that he appeared in another form unto two of them, as they walked, and went into the country [Mark 16:9-12].

Mark makes it very clear to us that he hadn't been following a chronological order in his Gospel. But now he says that this is the order. He is being chronological. He appeared first to Mary Magdalene. The disciples didn't believe Mary Magdalene at all. After that He appeared to two others, walking in the country. Luke gives us the account of that walk on the road to Emmaus.

And they went and told it unto the residue: neither believed they them.

Afterward he appeared unto the eleven as they sat at meat, and upbraided them with their unbelief and hardness of heart, because they believed not them which had seen him after he was risen [Mark 16:13,14].

You see that Mark does not include all the details but he does state the order in the events which he reports.

And he said unto them, Go ye into all the world, and preach the gospel to every creature [Mark 16:15].

This has been a Gospel of action. Now He's telling them to get into action! They are to go. And, by the way, He is saying to us today that we should be men and women of action for God. What are you doing today to get out the Word of God? That is our business, friends. You should be having some part in getting the Word of God *out* today.

He that believeth and is baptized shall be saved; but he that believeth not shall be damned [Mark 16:16].

He does not say that if you are not baptized you will be damned. He is not saying that baptism is necessary to salvation, but that the person who is saved will be baptized. It is the rejection of Christ which brings eternal damnation. "He that believeth on the Son hath everlasting life: and he that believeth not the Son shall not see life; but the wrath of God abideth on him" (John 3:36).

> **And these signs shall follow them that believe; In my name shall they cast out devils; they shall speak with new tongues;**
>
> **They shall take up serpents; and if they drink any deadly thing, it shall not hurt them; they shall lay hands on the sick, and they shall recover [Mark 16:17,18].**

If you want to accept any of these sign gifts, then you must take them all, brother. I'll be glad to prepare a formaldehyde cocktail if you think you can drink it. What am I trying to say? These signs have followed the preaching of the Gospel. But they are not signs to continue the preaching of the Gospel. They disappeared even in the early church, but they do manifest themselves on some primitive mission frontiers even today. But if someone maintains that they are injunctions for today, then one must accept them all, even the drinking of a deadly poison. Even before the end of the first century, the sign gifts were no longer the credentials of the apostles. The test was correct doctrine (see 2 John 10). It is the Word of God that is the great sign in this hour.

> **So then after the Lord had spoken unto them, he was received up into heaven, and sat on the right hand of God.**
>
> **And they went forth, and preached every where, the Lord working with them, and confirming the word with signs following. Amen. [Mark 16:19,20].**

This is Mark's brief statement of the great fact of the ascension and the present ministry of Jesus at the right hand of God. The disciples *did* go out to carry the Gospel to every creature, and the Lord *did* work with them and confirmed the Word with signs which they performed.

This is the Gospel of action. May we be men and women of *action* for God!

BIBLIOGRAPHY
(Recommended for Further Study)

English, E. Schuyler. *Studies in Mark's Gospel*. New York, NY: Our Hope Publishers, 1943.

Grassmick, John D. *Mark*. Chicago, IL: Moody Press, 1984.

Hendriksen, William. *Exposition of the Gospel According to Mark*. Grand Rapids, MI: Baker Book House, 1975.

Hiebert, D. Edmond. *Mark: A Portrait of a Servant*. Chicago, IL: Moody Press, 1974.

Ironside, H. A. *Addresses on the Gospel of Mark*. Neptune, NJ: Loizeaux Brothers.

Kelly, William. *An Exposition of the Gospel of Mark*. Addison, IL: Bible Truth Publishers, 1907.

Morgan, G. Campbell. *The Gospel According to Mark*. Old Tappan, NJ: Fleming H. Revell Co., 1927.

Pentecost, J. Dwight. *The Words and Works of Jesus Christ*. Grand Rapids, MI: Zondervan Publishing House, 1981.

Scroggie, W. Graham. *The Gospel of Mark*. Grand Rapids, MI: Zondervan Publishing House, n.d.

Scroggie, W. Graham. *A Guide to the Gospels*. London, England: Pickering & Inglis, 1948.

Von Ryn, August. *Meditations in Mark*. Neptune, NJ: Loizeaux Brothers, 1957.

Vos, Howard F. *Mark, A Study Guide Commentary*. Grand Rapids, MI: Zondervan Publishing House, 1978.

Wuest, Kenneth S. *Mark in the Greek New Testament for English Readers*. Grand Rapids, MI: Wm. B. Eerdmans Publishing Co., 1950.